You, Me an

Reader Reviews

"A really great book for anyone's spiritual journey. Teens, adults, everyone could use it for interior searching and growth."

"Gentle, thoughtful, and encouraging. A prayerful, simple, and light approach to complicated things."

"There's something here for everyone. I like that I could pick the topics that caught my eye. The chapter titles intrigued me."

"A+. I can't wait to get my own copy so I can really get into the reflective questions. That's my way of growing internally, spiritually."

"I love the title. The three part of it makes me think of the blessed Trinity. Yes."

*To my father, who left this world so unexpectedly
and my mother, who carried on so heroically.*

CONTENTS

CONTENTS

Preface

The second period bell rang. The freshman high school students hustled by each other to get to their seats. Once calm settled across the classroom, the teacher stood and approached the chalk-stained blackboard. It was actually green. She wrote, "Speech 101." A commotion arose in the back of the room as a student slipped from his seat and scurried out the classroom door. At least one student always starts out in the wrong classroom.

The teacher took a calming breath and announced, "Welcome to speech class 101. We'll start off by each of you telling the rest of the class who you are. Who's first?"

A student in the front of the room, the one annoying student who is always first to enthusiastically raise his hand to answer a question, promptly said, "I'll go first." The teacher nodded and invited him to the front of the room to address the class. The teacher settled behind her desk, folded her arms, and awaited the inaugural speech of the new school year.

The student proudly surveyed the class and began speaking. "The philosopher, Socrates, said, 'Know thyself.' This is what I'll talk about." When he continued to explain what the philosopher meant, the other students looked puzzled, and the teacher rose from her desk.

"Excuse me, Gary," she interrupted with more than a little sarcasm. "That's not what I meant." She asked Gary to take his seat. She waved another student to the front. Within seconds, the young girl gave her name, and boasted about her family and hobbies.

When she finished, the teacher offered a smile of vindication as she nodded towards Gary as if to say, "That's what I meant, dummy." He nodded with a slight smile as he slouched in his seat, embarrassed for life.

Yes, that student was me. That was my first attempt to impress upon an audience the importance of knowing oneself. And yes, here I go again.

Have you asked yourself a very simple yet difficult and provocative question? Have you ever asked yourself: Who am I? Many people would offer their name as an answer. Others might add a descriptive regarding gender, nationality, race, or religion. Still others might give their "elevator speech," citing their profession and how they benefit clients.

While all could be true, these answers simply scratch the surface. Beneath that surface rests many offshoots of that question. Philosophers, psychologists, theologians, poets, and many others have spent countless hours considering these questions. Why am I here? What is my purpose in life? What am I like? What is my self-concept? What do others see in me? The list goes on. As a Christian life coach, I help clients discover their own answers from a faith-based, Bible-based perspective.

My intention in writing *You, Me, and God Make Three,* is to provide you opportunities to increase your self-knowledge, reflect on your personal experiences, and enhance your spiritual awareness and intimacy with the triune God as you continue on your Christian walk.

Holy Spirit, be present with all who read this book as you have been present throughout its creation. Give them insight and wisdom on how to apply the ideas and principles you have laid on my heart to share.

Introduction

At the beginning of a coaching relationship, I tell the client there are three parties involved in my Christian life coaching sessions. Obviously, the client and myself are present at each session. The third person, I stress to the client, is the Lord our God. I tell the client from the first session going forward, "It's you, me, and God make three."

I now invite you, the reader, to join in an eclectic conversation as we walk with God, and I share insights and quotes he has laid upon my heart through my experiences regarding key areas of personal, professional, and spiritual growth, and the Christian experience.

Hopefully you will have an active role in the conversation, answering application questions and meditating on thought-provoking scriptures and quotes that will help you discover more about yourself, how to make the changes you want to make, and how to be more of what God wants you to be as you progress in your Christian walk.

How will the triune God be involved? God the Father will be present as we consider and explore Old Testament scriptures. God the Son, Jesus Christ, will speak through New Testament scriptures. And God the Holy Spirit will bless us with his presence as we call upon him together for wisdom and discernment. Also expect dozens of well-known philosophers, theologians, authors, speakers, entertainers, and other public figures to walk with us offering words of wisdom.

There are 52 thought-provoking readings in this book. Each reading includes a personal reflection (In My Words), relevant scriptures (In God's Words), inspirational quotes (In the Words of Others), questions and applications (In Your Words), space for journaling (In Your Journal), and a suggested prayer for sharing (Say It. Pray It. Share It.).

I encourage you to share the ending prayer with others, as I've been doing on social media for many months. I hope the combination of these elements will encourage an inner dialogue as you proceed on your Christian walk.

Develop your own reading plan. Spend some time with each selection, reflecting on its content, using it for daily or weekly meditations, or reading several selections at a time and revisiting them as needed. It is not a book to be read in one or two sittings and tucked away on a self.

I sincerely hope you will be blessed as you walk with me, the Lord, and the others who joined us along the way.

The Song: *"Walk Like a Christian"*

In My Words

Yes, you're correct. The song is *Walk Like an Egyptian*. Now think about this. What would the lyrics be of a song called *Walk Like a Christian*?

Would it be a catchy tune that would reverberate in your head and conjure up images of people sitting in church raising their hands in praise? Would it be a more measured, thoughtful piece raising images of someone deep in prayer or reading the Bible? Or would it have a more dramatic, somber rhythm invoking images of volunteers feeding hungry people or assisting an elderly person in a nursing home?

The lyrics could summon up images of people like you and me worshiping the triune God, learning about him through his Word, communicating with him through prayer, obediently living according to his commandments, or serving his hurting people.

You live your God-given purpose horizontally.

The cross of Christ is a reminder of how much the Lord our God loves us. It's also a fitting reminder of the two dimensions of what it means to walk like a Christian. Think of the vertical beam of the cross as representing the intimate relationship we should have with God. Having an obediently intimate relationship with the triune God grounds our Christian walk in a solid spiritual reality just as the vertical beam of the cross was buried deep in the ground of Golgotha.

The horizontal beam of the cross represents our Christian walk, how we are living out the Gospel in our lives, being a positive influence in all dimensions of our life. It is how we live out our God-given purpose horizontally, serving him as living witnesses of his love in service.

Spiritually, our Christian walk should be a process of continuous spiritual formation and sanctification, a growing in spiritual maturity that witnesses to others what it means to be a child of God.

Do you recall movies like *Grease* in which the "cool" guys like John Travolta strutted their way across the screen as girls swooned? Wouldn't it be "cool" if when you and I walked down the street heads would turn and onlookers would say, "Look, they walk like Christians!"

In God's Words

Trust in the LORD with all your heart and lean not on your own understanding; in all your ways submit to him, and he will make your paths straight. (Proverbs 3:5-6)

Walk in obedience to all that the LORD your God has commanded you, so that you may live and prosper and prolong your days in the land that you will possess. (Deuteronomy 5:33)

But if we walk in the light, as he is in the light, we have fellowship with one another, and the blood of Jesus, his Son, purifies us from all sin. (1 John 1:7)

Also read: Psalm 119:105, Proverbs 19:17, 1 Peter 4:10

In the Words of Others

"For every genuine testimony of love shown by us to those around us, by its very nature tends towards the cross of Christ." John M. Sheehan

"**Look for every opportunity to encourage someone. You don't know who is wrestling with demons that could end his or her life that day. A kind word comes from God. Be brave enough to act on it.**" Aaron Behr

"**While God, for the most part, allows this cosmos [creation] to work according to the laws of nature, there is never a time when He is not actively involved in every detail of life.**" Charles R. Swindoll

In Your Words

How has God empowered you to positively affect others? What talents, experiences, and spiritual gifts?

How have you been a positive influence in your Christian walk in your various life spheres? At work on the job? In your social life? At home in your family?

What characteristics of Christ in the gospels do you see manifested in your life? How have they influenced others?

What relationships have helped your Christian walk? What areas of sin have slowed down progress?

In Your Journal

Say It. Pray It. Share It.

Lord Jesus, help me obediently walk the straight and narrow path you have mapped out for me, so I might be a witness to others. Help me to be alert for opportunities to better serve you.

What Kind of Tree Are You?

In My Words

Driving down a country road one day, I marveled at how the trees lining the road on either side reminded me of people lining a parade route. There were tall trees and small trees. Handsome trees and plain-looking trees. Some were well dressed. Others had a minimal amount of leaves.

They also could have been soldiers or civilians honoring a soldier or first responder for their service along a parade route. And when the wind began blowing, the arbor army began waving, some forward, others backward and side to side.

As I passed through that tree-lined gauntlet I wondered which one of those trees could represent me. I glanced at my Bible sitting on the seat beside me and started thinking about trees in the scriptures. What does Scripture have to say about trees being part of God's plan? What would Scripture say about trees and my Christian walk?

Trees play important supporting roles in the Bible.

The word "tree" has no formal definition. However, we all know one when we see one. Tradition has it that trees represent nature, life, and fertility. When we think of trees, we think of peace, harmony, and strength. We often marvel at how they withstand storms and mighty winds. And we can be thankful for trees when we relax on a backyard wooden swing.

Trees of all kinds play supporting roles in the Bible. Some are major supporting actors. Others are character actors adding context to the scene. Still others are on the periphery as part of the crowd. There are over 56 verses in which a tree of some kind is mentioned.

Isn't it interesting that you can often tell what type of tree it is just by looking at the shape and color of their leaves, or the kind of fruit it bears? In the same way, those around you can tell what kind of person, and more importantly, what kind of Christian you are, by looking at how you act and the kind of fruit you bear.

In God's Words

No good tree bears bad fruit, nor does a bad tree bear good fruit. Each tree is recognized by its own fruit. People do not pick figs from thorn bushes, or grapes from briers.
(Luke 6:43-44)

The ax is already at the root of the trees, and every tree that does not produce good fruit will be cut down and thrown into the fire. (Matthew 3:10)

Also Read: Proverbs 13:12, Ezekiel 17:24, Daniel 4:10-12

In the Words of Others

"We can learn a lot from trees: they're always grounded, but never stop reaching heavenward."
Everett Mamor

"Life without love is like a tree without blossoms or fruit." Kahil Gibran

"God writes the Gospel not in the Bible alone, but also on trees, and in the flowers and clouds and stars."
Martin Luther

In Your Words

What kind of tree are you? Consider these references to trees in the Bible and the kind of tree or trees that best represent you and the fruit you bear as a Christian.

Are you a "tree planted by the water that sends out its roots by the stream. It does not fear when heat comes; its leaves are always green. It has no worries in a year of drought and never fails to bear fruit." (Jeremiah 17:8)

Perhaps you are a tree of the forest that sings for "joy before the Lord?" (1 Chronicles 16:33)

Are you a hopeful and resilient tree? "At least there is hope for a tree: If it is cut down, it will sprout again, and its new shoots will not fail." (Job 14:7)

Are you a healing tree, one whose "leaves of the tree are for the healing of the nations?" (Revelation 22:2)

Are you a trusting tree? "But I am like an olive tree flourishing in the house of God. I trust in God's unfailing love for ever and ever." (Psalm 52:8)

If you're in your later years, are you still making a difference in people's lives? "They will still bear fruit in old age, they will stay fresh and green," (Psalm 92:14)

Or, are you a "bad tree" that "bears bad fruit?" (Matthew 7:17)

In Your Journal

Say it. Pray it. Share it.

Father God, you gave us trees to encourage us to plant good seeds, establish deep roots, grow tall and strong, and spread our branches, bearing good fruit. I pray I will withstand the winds of adversity and bear good fruit.

Head, Heart, Hands Happiness

In My Words

The 1891 version of the *Baltimore Catechism* asks, "Why did God make you?" It answers, "God made me to know Him, to love Him, and to serve Him in this world and to be happy with Him forever in heaven."[1] The document then asks a question regarding salvation, "What must we do to save our souls?" The text answers, "To save our souls, we must worship God by faith, hope, and charity; that is, we must believe in Him, hope in Him, and love Him with all our heart."[2]

The key sentence as it pertains to our Christian walk reads, "God made me to know Him, to love Him, and to serve Him in this world and to be happy with Him forever in heaven." Put another way, we must learn about God, love him in an intimate relationship, and live our lives in service. We must use our heads, our hearts, and our hands. And when we know, love, and serve God, it is Jesus Christ we know, love, and serve.

We give God our head, our heart, and our hands.

We know God by his Word, through reading, studying, and meditating on scripture, especially the Gospel of Jesus Christ. We love God by having a vibrant intimate relationship with him through prayer. We serve him by serving others as Jesus calls us to do. This three-fold reality is the central message of the Gospel we should obediently pursue in whatever way God leads us. Ultimately, if we know, love and serve God, we worship him by believing in him, loving him with all our heart, and hoping for the salvation of our souls.

In God's Words

All Scripture is God-breathed and is useful for teaching, rebuking, correcting and training in righteousness, so that the servant of God may be thoroughly equipped for every good work. (2 Timothy 3:16-17)

He answered, "Love the Lord your God with all your heart and with all your soul and with all your strength and with all your mind and, love your neighbor as yourself." (Luke 10:27)

Each of you should use whatever gift you have received to serve others, as faithful stewards of God's grace in its various forms. If anyone speaks, they should do so as one who speaks the very words of God. If anyone serves, they should do so with the strength God provides, so that in all things God may be praised through Jesus Christ. To him be the glory and the power for ever and ever. Amen. (1 Peter 4:10-11)

Also read: Samuel 12:24, Matthew 5:8, John 1:18

In the Words of Others

"Only by aligning our wills with God's is full happiness found." Neal A. Maxwell

"There's a difference between knowing God and knowing about God. When you truly know God, you have energy to serve Him, boldness to share Him, and contentment in Him." J. I. Packer

"Don't shine so others can see you. Shine so that through you, others can see Him." C.S. Lewis

In Your Words

Describe the ways you try to know Jesus Christ better. Are there other ways you can do this?

Do you have a daily routine that helps you grow in your knowledge of Jesus Christ? If so, describe it.

Describe ways you display your love of Jesus Christ and experience intimacy with him. How do you feel spiritually then? Do you feel energized spiritually? Why?

In Your Journal

Say It. Pray It. Share It.

Lord Jesus, help me to learn more about you and your holy will, to have an intimate relationship of love with you, and to serve you by serving others according to your will.

Three Ways You Co-Create with God

In My Words

God created the world for a purpose. Philosophers, theologians and many others have speculated on exactly why the Lord, our God, created the heavens and the earth in the very beginning as described in the Book of Genesis. Perhaps he was bored since there was literally nothing to do. Scripture tells us why he created man and woman, but God alone knows his purpose for creating the world.

Have you thought much about the passage in Genesis 1:26 in which it clearly states God created mankind in his own image, his own likeness? That's right. That awesome statement is there in the beginning of the Bible. You and I are created in God's own image. And with that truth comes an equally awesome responsibility.

If God was a creator, the ultimate creator, then you and I are creators. The wonderful irony is that we are responsible for doing our parts as co-creators and coworkers in accomplishing God's purpose even though the reason for his ultimate creation, the world itself, remains a mystery to us.

Invest the gifts God has blessed you with wisely.

There are three ways we co-create and are co-workers with God. As the Book of Genesis makes clear, we are to take care of his creation. "Let us make mankind in our image, in our likeness, so that they may rule over the fish in the sea and the birds in the sky, over the livestock and all the wild animals, and over all the creatures that move along the ground." As God created man and woman after seeing the need for relationship, we create the world around us in relationships. Most importantly, God has given each of us

19

the opportunity to help him create his Kingdom here on earth by giving us his son, Jesus Christ, and the Holy Spirit.

You create your world by influencing the world around you. As someone made in the image of God, you have the power to influence yourself and the world around you by the choices you make and the actions you take.

You can be a positive or negative influence in how you take care of God's earth, engage in relationships with your fellow human beings, and in helping to build his kingdom on earth. Everyone can be an influence in this way, using, not using, or abusing the resources and gifts God gives us.

God works in different ways through each of us. We have all been given different gifts, abilities, and experiences. We should invest these wisely, honoring God as we bless, encourage, and strengthen others in love.

His purpose for creating the world may remain a mystery, but God's purpose for creating us is clear. As we faithfully serve him, we use our gifts to glorify him, taking care of his creation, and attending to his Kingdom on earth by serving others.

In God's Words

The earth is the LORD's, and everything in it, the world, and all who live in it; (Psalm 24:1)

Each of you should use whatever gift you have received to serve others, as faithful stewards of God's grace in its various forms. (1 Peter 4:10)

For we are co-workers in God's service; you are God's field, God's building. (1 Corinthians 3:9)

Also Read: 2 Chronicles 15:7, 2 Corinthians 5:20, Mark 4:26

In the Words of Others

"You are called to care for creation, not only as responsible citizens, but also as followers of Christ."
Pope Francis

"God intends...our care of creation to reflect our love for the creator." John Stott

"We do not want a church that will move with the world. We want a church that will move the world."
G. K. Chesterton

In Your Words

Recall times when you made a difference in caring for God's earth, serving others, and contributing to building God's Kingdom on earth.

How do you feel about this? Will this change what you do going forward?

Name three ways you can be a positive influence in your family, social, and professional life spheres.

In Your Journal

Say it. Pray it. Share it.

Father God, I thank you for creating me and the world. I accept the challenge to take care of your creation, to foster positive relationships, and to help build your Kingdom on earth.

Is Your Personality a Fragrance of Christ?

In My Words

I always have to stop and smell the flowers. Sometimes I'm overwhelmed by the wonderful scents that emerge, just like the aroma of a fine wine rising from a glass. At other times, the scent is less appealing and even undetectable. The same can be said about scents given off when a woman wearing perfume or a man wearing cologne passes by.

Investment guru Charles Schwab once said personality is to a man what perfume is to a flower. I'm sure he would also apply this to women. And if you think about people you've met over the years, my guess is you would agree. A person's personality does project a social and emotional fragrance for good or bad.

Actions give off an aroma of Christ to God, others.

The word "personality" comes from the Latin word "persona." It refers to a mask worn by performers who wanted to project a certain role, disguising their identity. Our personality is how we might describe ourselves and how others see us. It is the collection of thoughts, feelings, and behaviors that make us unique.

We often look at other people and assess their personalities. Consciously or unconsciously, we see a recognizable order to their behavior. Their personality influences how they move and respond to their environment, as well as causing us to respond in certain ways.

Actions do speak louder than words. Take for example, body language. Researchers have determined that much of the communication that takes place between individuals is through body language.

The apostle Paul knew the importance of how people can be influenced by the way we act, and how our inner selves emerge through our personality. This is why he stressed several times in his letters the importance of how actions displaying love can be a testimony to others, an aroma of what it means to be a follower of Christ, and a living sacrifice to the Father. As Christians, we are both the medium of God's love and compassion, and his message to others, by the way we act and the "fragrance" we emit.

In God's Words

For we are to God the pleasing aroma of Christ among those who are being saved and those who are perishing.   (2 Corinthians 2:15)

Follow God's example, therefore, as dearly loved children and walk in the way of love, just as Christ loved us and gave himself up for us as a fragrant offering and sacrifice to God. (Ephesians 5:1-2)

In the same way, let your light shine before others, that they may see your good deeds and glorify your Father in heaven. (Matthew 5:16)

Also Read: Genesis 8:21, Psalm 139:14, 1 Corinthians 13:1-13

In the Words of Others

"I hold that a strongly marked personality can influence descendants for generations." Beatrix Potter

"When you are joyful, when you say yes to life and have fun and project positivity all around you, you become a sun in the center of every constellation, and people want to be near you." Shannon L. Alder

"If you would convince a man that he does wrong, do right. But do not care to convince him. Men will believe what they see. Let them see." Henry David Thoreau

In Your Words

Have there been times your personality has given off a less favorable scent as a Christian? What could you have changed?

Think of a person who gives off a positive aroma of the love of God? Describe how he or she is a living message from God.

Think of a person who claims to be a Christian but delivers mixed messages by his or her actions. Why do you think so?

In Your Journal

Say It. Pray It. Share It.

Holy Spirit, be at my side throughout my days reminding me and encouraging me to act in a way that is a sweet aroma to others and the Father, giving him all honor and glory.

Unleash the Power of the Gospel in Your Life

In My Words

The symphony hall was packed with a sold-out crowd. The anticipation was palpable. The lights dimmed. You could feel the audience hold its collective breath waiting for the conductor to tap his baton on the podium and alert the impressively stoic orchestra that they were about to perform the magnificent Fifth Symphony of Beethoven.

The immaculately dressed conductor embraced the baton and stood there staring at the score. The seconds turned into minutes, and the minutes into an hour. It's a good thing the audience began taking collective breaths because the conductor continued to stare at the score, never to raise his baton. The powerful symphony, penned by one of the greatest composers of all time, remained thousands of black notes on sheet music pages. The power of Beethoven's Fifth Symphony remained unleashed.

Live the Gospel of Jesus Christ in love and service.

Have you ever thought about how the power of the Gospel of Jesus Christ is not unleashed in our lives until it is performed? Paul writes in Romans that the Gospel is the power of God. But that power is never unleashed in our lives if we read and study the Gospel without living it.

To help us live out the Gospel, we need to condense it into a core message that we can ingrain in our minds, and subsequently in our emotions, so our actions consciously and unconsciously reflect Gospel truth as it applies to our daily lives. What exactly is this core message?

25

The Gospel has three core life principles, all of which center around love. First, God loves us, and because he is love itself, he loves us without limit, unconditionally. The ultimate demonstration of the depth of his love for us was the sacrifice of his Son on the cross. Jesus went to the cross for us out of pure obedience and love.

The next core life principle of the Gospel of Jesus Christ is our love for God. His unconditional love for us requires us to love him unconditionally. We must strive to maintain an intimate relationship with him, one that requires unconditional obedience and heart-felt repentance should that relationship be breached in any way.

Finally, we should not only love our neighbor as ourselves. We should love others as God loves us and as we love him. Our love of others should be unconditional and sacrificial as God's love for us. It should be based on service, allowing God's love for us to manifest itself through the presence of Jesus Christ in us and the power of the Holy Spirit.

In God's Words

In the same way, let your light shine before others, that they may see your good deeds and glorify your Father in heaven. (Matthew 5:16)

What good is it, my brothers and sisters, if someone claims to have faith but has no deeds? Can such faith save them?
(James 2:14)

In the same way, faith by itself, if it is not accompanied by action, is dead. (James 2:17)

Also read: Hebrews 11:8, Ephesians 2:8-9, Titus 2:7

In the Words of Others

"The gospel is not a doctrine of the tongue, but of life. It cannot be grasped by reason and memory only, but it is fully understood when it possesses the whole soul and penetrates to the inner recesses of the heart." John Calvin

"We become examples of the believers by living the gospel of Jesus Christ in word, in conversation, in charity, in spirit, in faith, and in purity. As we do so, our lights will shine for others to see." Thomas S. Monson

"The Gospel is not a mere message of deliverance, but a canon of conduct; it is not a theology to be accepted, but it is ethics to be lived. It is not to be believed only, but it is to be taken into life as a guide." Alexander MacLaren

In Your Words

Describe how you have experienced the love and power of God and his Son, Jesus Christ, in your life.

How have you lived the Gospel up until now? What changes do you think you should make in the future?

Explain in your own words the core message of the Gospel of Jesus Christ.

Write a summary of how you will unleash the power of the Gospel in your life on a small note card. Visit it daily.

In Your Journal

Say It. Pray It. Share It.

Lord Jesus, help me begin each day knowing I can unleash the power of your Gospel by loving others as you love me. Holy Spirit, give me the strength and courage to fulfill this divine mission.

How Big Is Your God?

In My Words

How big is your God? Do you keep him in a little box tucked away in a corner on a shelf, only to be opened when needed? Is he a short, meek fellow always sitting in the hall waiting to be let into the part of your life you keep off limits? Is he a small, barely visible figure on a distant mountain top you can only see with binoculars? Or is he for you, as the song says, an AWESOME God?

How you size up God has a lot to do with the way you relate to him. Whether you see God as small enough to be tucked into a box, meek enough to be kept out of all of your life's rooms, or barely visible on a distant mountain top, you can still relate to him as a friend, and that is important. But your God is more than a boxed friend, a meek friend, a distant friend. He is your God, an AWESOME God, an AWESOME friend.

How big is your God? You don't need a degree in theology to figure that out. He is big enough to have created the world. He is big enough to care for it, including you and me. He is big enough to know every hair on our head. He was also big enough to be humble, to die on the cross for us.

God offers supernatural surplus and blessings.

How we view God affects how we pray to him. We miniaturize God by coming before him with weak and meek prayers. True, we are all sinful human beings who should humbly come before him on our knees. But our God appreciates it when we come before him with big faith and big expectations. He is a God of abundance, supernatural surplus, and bountiful blessings. He is a God who we should love just for being who he is.

Whether we come before God regarding our health, our wealth, our families, or our careers, we need to see what he can will for us with big vision and big expectations. If we pray in his will, he will deliver according to his riches. When we ask for a little, God will honor our request.

In God's Words

Great is the LORD and most worthy of praise; his greatness no one can fathom. (Psalm 145:3)

Oh, the depth of the riches of the wisdom and knowledge of God! How unsearchable his judgments, and his paths beyond tracing out! (Romans 11:33)

And God is able to bless you abundantly, so that in all things at all times, having all that you need, you will abound in every good work. (2 Corinthians 9:8)

Also read: Psalm 139:7-12, Jeremiah 10:10, Matthew 7:7, Romans 8:37-39

In the Words of Others

"Stop limiting God with small requests. We serve a big God who knows no limits." Pastor John Hagee

"Sometimes when we get overwhelmed, we forget how big God is." A.W. Tozer

"I will not talk to God about how big my problems are. I will talk to my problems about how big my God is. This is my declaration." Joel Osteen

In Your Words

Create a brief "elevator speech" describing God as you see him. Don't be afraid to boast about God, and what he can do for you.

Describe the prayer you might use when asking for something big or when facing an insurmountable challenge in your life. Think big.

Get into the habit of getting up in the morning and marveling at the magnificent world God created. Read Psalm 95 and others that praise his handiwork before starting your day.

Do you spend time with God, appreciating who he is and not what he can do for you? Describe how that makes you feel.

In Your Journal

Say It. Pray It. Share It.

Father God, help me remember you are bigger than any problem or challenge I face. Help me to come before you with great expectations, but always submitting to your holy and true will.

Having "Whatever" Faith

In My Words

One of my jobs in the steel mill was operating a larry car on railroad tracks that carried a ladle filled with molten pig iron. A huge overhead crane would grab the ladle and pour its content into an open-hearth furnace. While this was going on, I would often sit on a bench and peer into a nearby furnace.

I would think about three biblical characters who roamed around in a furnace, and who survived the experience according to Daniel 3, Shadrach, Meshach, and Abednego. These were the three Hebrew men in the Book of Daniel who were thrown into a fiery furnace by Nebuchadnezzar, king of Babylon. They refused to bow down to the king's image. A fourth figure joined them as they were preserved from harm. The king saw four men walking in the flames and said, "the fourth looks like a son of the gods."

God is at our side in our personal fiery furnaces.

Thinking back on my thoughts at that time, the passage in the Daniel story that most fascinates me today is what they said in response to the king. These three Hebrew men stood up to the king and gave him a big spiritual "whatever." Whatever the king was about to do to them, they stood firm on their confidence in the God who would do what he promises to do.

This was not a mere shrugging of the shoulders by a young teenager telling his mom or dad "whatever." This was a powerful demonstration of absolute reliance on what the scriptures say about God's supreme power, and how he can deliver us from the fiery furnace of our own everyday problems and challenges.

This is a wonderful example of reliance on God's power. But I wonder how the three Hebrews really felt as they walked into Nebuchadnezzar's furnace. I imagine that like you and I would have reacted, they experienced moments of hesitation, doubt, or even terror. After all, like us, they were human, despite their great faith in God.

We should all take heart that like Shadrach, Meshach and Abednego, we can face whatever life and Satan brings our way with the assurance that God will be at our side in our personal fiery furnaces, even when we have less than perfect faith.

It is in pressing on, that we show our faith and God is glorified. And unlike these three Hebrews who defied an evil king, we have Jesus Christ, to not only stand at our side in our times of trouble, but to be in us, strengthening us. This should give us a great sense of freedom, a spiritual "whatever" attitude.

In God's Words

When you pass through the waters, I will be with you; and when you pass through the rivers, they will not sweep over you. When you walk through the fire, you will not be burned; the flames will not set you ablaze. (Isaiah 43:2)

Do not be anxious about anything, but in every situation, by prayer and petition, with thanksgiving, present your requests to God. And the peace of God, which transcends all understanding, will guard your hearts and your minds in Christ Jesus. (Philippians 4:6-7)

Also read: Deuteronomy 31:10, Psalm 46:1-2, Daniel 3:15-18

In the Words of Others

"God doesn't call us to be comfortable. He calls us to trust him so completely that we are unafraid to put ourselves in situations where we will still be in trouble even if He doesn't come through." Francis Chan

"Our heavenly Father understands our disappointment, suffering, pain, fear, and doubt. He is always there to encourage our hearts and help us understand that He's sufficient for all of our needs. When I accepted this as an absolute truth in my life, I found that my worrying stopped." Charles Stanley

In Your Words

Can you recall a time in your life when it seemed like God was your only hope? If yes, describe how you felt at the time.

Recall a time when you should have sought God's help, but turned elsewhere and regretted it, finally turning to God for support. What were you thinking at the time?

Describe the kind of personal faith in God you have. Is it the kind of faith you place in God regardless of the outcome? Or is it the kind of faith that relies on favorable outcomes?

Visit the scriptures and identify other characters who demonstrated spiritual "whatever" faith in their Lord and God, after leaving their fate in his hands. Visit Genesis 50:20, Ruth 1:16-18, 2 Kings 1:15.

In Your Journal

Say It. Pray It. Share It.

Lord Jesus, strengthen my faith so that no matter what I face in life, I will trust you, love you, praise you, and thank you. Holy Spirit, give me strength to face each day with confidence.

I Wanna Be Like Me

In My Words

In 1992, Gatorade aired one of the most memorable commercials of all time, "Be Like Mike," or as it became known based on its lyrics, "I Wanna Be Like Mike."

It's part of our human nature to "wanna be" like someone else. When we're young, we want to be like our older siblings or parents. As we grow older, we look up to and try to be like sports figures, entertainers, and other famous people. Advertisers thrive on their ability to convince us that our worth and self-identify is based on looking like the physically perfect and stylistically "cool" actors in their commercials.

There are two people we should strive to be like. The first is Jesus Christ. Admittedly, this is a tall order. The second is being like ourselves. This is also a tall order. It seems like the whole world wants us to be someone else, someone better, someone different than who we really are.

What characteristics did Christ display?

As Christians, we endeavor to be like Christ and in turn remain true to who God the Father made us. But what characteristics did Christ display? The answer to this question tells us who we need to be.

Jesus spent time in the emotional valleys with sinners and broken people. He also dedicated time to prayer, a practice that energized him in his ministry. He forgave those who needed forgiveness and encouraged them to move on, loved and renewed. He saw their heart, not as others saw them.

As the red-lettered words in certain editions of the Bible show, Jesus was a man of many words. But he was also a man of action who brought those words to life. He was knowledgeable in the Law, but followed a higher law, being obedient to his Father, even unto death. Instead of being served, he was a servant, expecting his followers to also serve.

Most importantly, he was powered by and lead by the Holy Spirit. He was not only God in the flesh. If you read between the lines of the New Testament, when he walked into a room, a synagogue, a crowd, and the judgement seats of local Roman officials, all knew he was more than a good person and teacher.

As Christians who should be dedicated in our Christian walk to trying to be as Christ-like as possible, we have one model to guide us in our efforts to be renewed in our minds and truly who our creator wants us to be. It is Jesus Christ.

We should "wanna be" who God made us to be, not what the world tells us we should be. Let's say it together: I "wanna be" like me, the me God wants me to be.

In God's Words

But the LORD said to Samuel, "Do not consider his appearance or his height, for I have rejected him. The LORD does not look at the things people look at. People look at the outward appearance, but the LORD looks at the heart." (1 Samuel 16:7)

You were taught, with regard to your former way of life, to put off your old self, which is being corrupted by its deceitful desires; to be made new in the attitude of your minds; and to put on the new self, created to be like God in true righteousness and holiness. (Ephesians 4:22-24)

Also read: 1 Corinthians 2:16, 1 Peter 3:3-4, Matthew 5:48

In the Words of Others

"Be yourself; everyone else is already taken." Oscar Wilde

"Always be a first-rate version of yourself and not a second-rate version of someone else." Judy Garland

"To be yourself in a world that is constantly trying to make you something else is the greatest accomplishment." Ralph Waldo Emerson

In Your Words

What would people say about your character and how you act as a Christian?

If you described your "new self" in an effort to be more Christ-like, how would it be based on Jesus in the gospels?

If you could choose one person to be like, who would that be, and why? Is that person walking the Christian walk?

In Your Journal

Say It. Pray It. Share It.

Father God, you made me a perfect version of me. I pray I will try to live every day as Jesus Christ would live, giving you thanks and praise for how special you made me.

Contradiction: A Pathway to Discovering God

In My Words

A friend of mine received the results of an MRI. She told me the test results were negative. She said because the results were negative, they confirmed she was very sick. I smiled and gave her the good news, that negative test results were a good thing, that negative was positive and positive was negative.

This experience demonstrates what I call simple contradiction. It is simply the use of terms or combination of terms that at face value seem to represent their opposite. Another example is a combination of two street signs I saw one day. One sign read "Do Not Enter." A sign right beside it read "Entrance."

A loving God, love itself, is a God of judgement.

There are other examples of contradiction that are more complex, with a logical crease where they intersect, allowing discovery to occur. Failures become opportunities. Feeling useless while being useful. Being in a crowd and feeling alone. Giving up control to be free. And a corollary to that, needing laws to insure freedom. In each case, one ends where the other begins. One points to the other and gives the other meaning.

This is the case with what seems to be a significant contradiction of our Christian faith. The question: How can the God of infinite love who is love itself, also be the God of judgement, a God of wrath? This is a question often raised by non-believers who refuse to explore the place where these two attributes of God intersect, and where we find a pathway by which we can discover his true nature as the Triune God.

As a loving God, as love itself, he loves us despite what we do, and sent his Son to the cross to reconcile us to him. However, he still allows us to accept or reject his love. As a just God, he must judge us according to what we do when we reject his love through disobedience and sin.

Our heavenly Father loves us in the same way our earthly fathers should. As the loving source of our lives here on earth, our fathers should love us unconditionally for who we are and not necessarily what we do or don't do. On the other hand, they should hold us accountable, especially if our wrongdoing originates from or results in a rejection of their love.

What would be your view of God if you only had the Old Testament to rely on to help you reconcile how a God of love, love itself, could also be a God of wrath? The contradiction could still be understood, but the crease where God's two attributes intersect takes on a new meaning when the ultimate act of love on the cross reconciled the divide between God's love and his judgement.

In God's Words

For God so loved the world that he gave his one and only Son, that whoever believes in him shall not perish but have eternal life. (John 3:16)

And hope does not put us to shame, because God's love has been poured out into our hearts through the Holy Spirit, who has been given to us. (Romans 5:5)

Whoever does not love does not know God, because God is love. (1 John 4:8)

Also read: Psalm 9:8, Zephaniah 3:17, 1 John 2:1-29, Ephesians 1:3-8

In the Words of Others

"While the Bible's account of the flood is one of judgment, it is also one of mercy and salvation. Likewise, our future full-size evangelistic Noah's Ark will honor the Bible as God's word and not treat it as a pagan fable." Ken Ham

"God loves each of us as if there were only one of us." Saint Augustine

"It is not earthly rank, nor birth, nor nationality, nor religious privilege, which proves that we are member of the family of God; it is love, a love that embraces all humanity." Ellen G. White

In Your Words

Have there been times in your life when you experienced God's loving presence? Have there been times when you experienced his wrath? Describe why you felt that way in either or both cases.

How would you have explained this apparent contradiction to a non-believer before reading this reflection?

Has your view of God evolved over the years? Describe how and why?

Think about how the God of the Old Testament compares with the God of the New Testament, given Christ's death on the cross and resurrection. How would you describe the difference to a non-believer?

In Your Journal

Say It. Pray It. Share It.

Lord Jesus, I praise you and thank you for loving me for who I am and not what I do or not do. Caress me in your arms and love me, not because I deserve it, but because you are love.

God's Reverse Psychology

In My Words

I've heard a number of people over the years comment about how Jesus was a practical psychologist. They cite the way he related to people and helped them work through their issues and problems, especially their sin. I would like to add another dimension to this idea.

Think of God the Father as the "great psychologist." In sending his Son into this world and requiring him to die on the cross, God performed the ultimate lesson of reverse psychology. He gave his Son in death so we might live and be with him for eternity.

By doing this, he taught us how to "die" to ourselves in service to others even as we have a need, and thereby reap benefits for ourselves. He taught us to plant a seed of service when we may be the ones in need. He taught us to empty our cups so he could generously refill them according to his spiritual riches.

As is made clear in the New Testament, each of us must die to ourselves in service of others. This is the way God's love will restore what was lost thousands of years ago in the garden. As a just God, he gave his Son on the cross to break the bond of sin and death. As a loving God, he gave his Son on the cross to show us how to individually restore the relationship broken by the Fall.

We are all servants in one way or another.

As Christ walked this earth, he continued his Father's practice of reverse psychology. In a number of scriptures, he tells us to be last so we might be first, to sacrifice that we might experience gain, not in a worldly since, but in a spiritual sense. The Beatitudes is a great example.

St. Francis of Assisi's Peace Prayer echoes this idea, "It is in dying that we are born to eternal life." The prayer suggests when we empty ourselves by giving to others, we make room for the Lord's blessings. Give love and you will be loved. Console and you will be consoled. Understand and you will be understood.

We are all servants in one way or another. Some give generously of their time and other resources to help others in very unique ways. How we give depends on our God-given natural and spiritual gifts, the experiences that shape who we are, and the leading of the Holy Spirit.

Over the years, I've had the privilege of knowing dozens of volunteers who have given their time and other resources to serve others. To a person, they would tell you without hesitation, they believe they get more out of serving than those they serve. Many would describe it as a "win-win" for all involved. I call it God's reverse psychology at work.

In God's Words

You, my brothers and sisters, were called to be free. But do not use your freedom to indulge the flesh; rather, serve one another humbly in love. For the entire law is fulfilled in keeping this one command: "Love your neighbor as yourself." (Galatians 5:13-14)

And whoever wants to be first must be slave of all. For even the Son of Man did not come to be served, but to serve, and to give his life as a ransom for many. (Mark 10:44-45)

Sitting down, Jesus called the Twelve and said, "Anyone who wants to be first must be the very last, and the servant of all." (Mark 9:35)

Also read: Acts 20:35, Philippians 2:1-11, Luke 6:38

In the Words of Others

"The measure of man's greatness is not the number of servants he has, but the number of people he serves."
John Hagee

"The purpose of life is not to be happy. It is to be useful, to be honorable, to be compassionate, to have it make some difference that you have lived and lived well."
Ralph Waldo Emerson

"The purpose of human life is to serve, and to show compassion and the will to help others." Albert Schweitzer

In Your Words

In the last 30 days, who have you served by giving of your time or other resources, focusing on their needs and not your own?

Who have you thought about serving but never did? What were the reasons? In the next 30 days, how will you serve others?

Write down exactly who you will serve, how you will serve them, how committed you are to taking action, and the price you may have to pay to serve that person or persons. Sign it. Commit to it.

In Your Journal

Say It. Pray It, Share It.

Lord Jesus, I know you call me to serve you by serving others. However, today I hear you calling me to serve more and more. I hear you promising to fill me up as I empty myself in service.

Step by Step, Stumble by Stumble

In My Words

The Lord held my hand as we walked in the middle of a long two-lane road. Suddenly, as he and I kept walking forward, an image of me stumbling and falling, and the Lord picking me up with his right hand, began duplicating itself behind us hundreds of times in a quickly oscillating motion back to the horizon.

I thought, "The Lord is reminding me about how many times I've stumbled and fallen, and how many times he was there to pick me up." Then I woke up. I was dreaming.

I'm one of those people who have been blessed to have very vivid and detailed dreams. I also know when I'm in a dream and can often comment on what's happening while dreaming.

When I stumble, he extends his mighty right hand.

That you and I will stumble and fall many times throughout our lives is a given. Whether or not you are a believer, the Lord's right hand is always there to help lift you up. It's never a question of the Lord's willingness to lift us up. It's a matter of us accepting his freely given saving grace and walking in obedience at his side.

Even as someone who bears Christ's name, there is one thing we can count on, we will stumble and fall many, many times. How many times? To use a phrase Jesus uses in the Gospel of Matthew regarding forgiveness, we will stumble and fall "seventy times seven times," a phrase that symbolizes boundlessness.

Looking at this reality from a theological perspective, regardless of one's belief system, it's natural for us to think of wrongdoing, sin, and backsliding. But the Lord is also ready to lift us up when we lose a loved one, lose a job, suffer illness, and drift into despair and depression. It's often at these times when our faith falters and we fall prey to the evil one's creative devices. It's at these times, when falling before the Lord in prayer is a must.

I'm thankful the Lord was in my dream lifting me up with his right hand, for the extension of God's right hand is a common metaphor used in the Bible for his awesome power and omnipotence. What a blessing we have with the Lord at our side, every step of the way, every stumble of every day.

In God's Words

The LORD makes firm the steps of the one who delights in him; though he may stumble, he will not fall, for the LORD upholds him with his hand. (Psalm 37:23-24)

I was pushed back and about to fall, but the LORD helped me. (Psalm 118:13)

Humble yourselves, therefore, under God's mighty hand, that he may lift you up in due time. (1 Peter 5:6)

Also read: Proverbs 24:16, Samuel 22:37, 2 Corinthians 4:8-10

In the Words of Others

"When we fall down, God is always there to pick you back up." Joyce Meyer

"Never trust anyone completely but God. Love people but put your full trust only in God." Lawrence Welk

"Let your life reflect the faith you have in God. Fear nothing and pray about everything. Be strong, trust God's word, and trust the process." Germany Kent

In Your Words

Do you recall a time when you stumbled and fell spiritually, and how the Lord gave you strength to get back up? Describe how you believe he worked in your mind and heart at the time.

Can you cite times when you suffered a loss of some kind, and people and events helped you get through the tough times, and get back on your feet? Consider how the Lord played a role.

Recall the stories about Joseph in the Old Testament and Peter the apostle in the New Testament. How did they stumble? How did the Lord help them fulfill their ultimate destiny?

In Your Journal

Say It. Pray It. Share It.

Lord Jesus, I thank you for reminding me that I am totally dependent on you, especially when I stumble and fall. I pray I remember I will never be worthy of your help, but desperately need it.

Waiting to Celebrate with "Touchdown Jesus"

In My Words

One of the more entertaining parts of professional football in the U.S. are the end-zone celebrations. Once a player crosses the opponent's goal line with the football securely in his hands, all fun breaks out as he dances and prances around, spikes the football, and is tackled by cheering teammates in what resembles a rugby scrum or miniature mosh pit.

I drive past a cemetery every day that features a life-size, statue of Jesus alongside the road. One day it struck me that the statue reminded me of a referee signaling a touchdown with raised arms. Ever since that time, every time I pass that statue the name "Touchdown Jesus" comes to mind.

Head for the goal line and the Lord's raised arms.

Picture this. A faithful believer dies, enters heaven, and begins to dance and prance as angels and saints pile on in celebration. A glowing figure in an immaculate, brilliant white robe walks up with nail-marked hands and raises his arms to say, "You're a winner. Well done good and faithful servant!"

This picture is more elaborate than understanding the Christian's walk and life journey as Paul suggested, a good race. Regardless of the metaphor you use to picture the moment you pass from life on earth to an eternity in heaven, it's a time for excessive celebration without penalties.

There are principles to keep in mind as you strive to reach life's goal line and see the Lord with raised arms. A famous Vince Lombardi quote summarizes them. He said, "Football is like life---it requires perseverance, self-denial, hard work, sacrifice, dedication, and respect for authority."

As a Christian, you didn't get a trouble-free pass when you accepted Jesus Christ as your personal savior. You will never have a clear field in front of you where you can live your daily life without challenges blocking your progress or tempting distractions on the sideline that divert your attention from accomplishing your goals.

Your Christian walk involves being an example, showing perseverance in the face of temptations and struggles, self-denial and sacrifice in the service of others. It requires a dedication to keeping your eye on the goal, eternity with the Lord. It demands obedience, walking the straight and narrow path to the goal line, or as the Apostle Paul would have it, the finish line.

In God's Words

I have fought the good fight, I have finished the race, I have kept the faith. (2 Timothy 4:7)

Do you not know that in a race all the runners run, but only one gets the prize? Run in such a way as to get the prize. (1 Corinthians 9:24)

I press on toward the goal to win the prize for which God has called me heavenward in Christ Jesus. (Philippians 3:14)

Also read: Deuteronomy 20:14, Isaiah 40:31, Hebrews 12:11

In the Words of Others

"If you find a path with no obstacles, it probably doesn't lead anywhere." Frank A. Clark

"Obstacles are those frightful things you see when you take your eyes off the goal." Henry Ford

"If you wish to be out front, then act as if you were behind." Lao Tzu

"We can teach everything, but we can't teach integrity. We can't teach integrity, but we can lead by example." Jerry Oche

In Your Words

How have you been focused on the straight and narrow path towards the goal line, not being distracted?

Cite three examples of how self-control, self-denial, discipline, or obedience to God's commands and the Gospel have played a role in your Christian walk thus far.

In what ways have you been a good example for your family, friends, or coworkers who are struggling in their walk?

In Your Journal

Say It. Pray It. Share It.

Father God, I pray the Holy Spirit will be at my side as I strive to keep focused on who you want me to be. I look forward to Jesus welcoming me with open and raised arms.

Seeing the Extraordinary in the Ordinary

In My Words

One of my favorite movies about artists is *Lust for Life*, the movie starring Kirk Douglas as Vincent Van Gogh. I especially enjoy the scenes in which the artist packs up his canvas, paints, and brushes, and walks into the city and countryside to transform the ordinary into the extraordinary.

Through his artistry, Van Gogh transformed workers picking fruit in the fields, a landscape of winding roads along a country village, people eating potatoes, and even his own bedroom. His use of colors demonstrated a view of ordinary things and activities that transcended what others saw. He recognized the unseen and put it on canvas so others could see their own version of what he saw. They could stand back and see what he saw, and more.

> *God colors with supernatural brush strokes.*

God wants us to look at his creation and those around us with the eyes of faith, beyond the physical. He wants us to see the unseen with eyes of faith in the supernatural realm, the spiritual realm, where ordinary things and experiences take on a whole new meaning and perspective, his perspective. As Christians, the presence of Jesus Christ and the indwelling of the Holy Spirit in us allows us to know the spirit of God and gives us the potential to see with spiritual eyes as Van Gogh saw with an artist's eyes.

When you enter the spiritual realm through prayer, meditation on the Word, and focusing on the Lord our God in your quiet moments, your world is transformed in "God moments." You come to appreciate how God colors your ordinary world with supernatural brush strokes of eternal hues. You learn to appreciate how the tiniest of things and seemingly insignificant experiences have great meaning and relevance. You begin to recognize how momentous world events and celebrated accomplishments ultimately have little eternal significance and relevance.

You become more aware of the ways the Holy Spirit works in the world and in your life, who like the wind, moves people and events into position according to the Father's wishes, usually without fanfare, but never without power. The Spirit helps you participate in the Father's creativity through simple acts of obedience and meaningful acts of service. As he was present and active in the ultimate act of creation chronicled in Genesis, the Spirit is still the Father's creative touch in action, transforming the ordinary into the extraordinary.

In God's Words

Now faith is confidence in what we hope for and assurance about what we do not see. (Hebrews 11:1)

For our light and momentary troubles are achieving for us an eternal glory that far outweighs them all. So, we fix our eyes not on what is seen, but on what is unseen, since what is seen is temporary, but what is unseen is eternal. (2 Corinthians 4:17-18)

What we have received is not the spirit of the world, but the Spirit who is from God, so that we may understand what God has freely given us. This is what we speak, not in words taught us by human wisdom but in words taught by the Spirit, explaining spiritual realities with Spirit-taught words. (1 Corinthians 2:12-13)

Also Read: 1 Samuel 16:7, 2 Corinthians 5:7, 2 Hebrews 1:14

In the Words of Others

"Appearances are a glimpse of the unseen." Anaxagoras

"Much of the important work of God is unseen in the eyes of the world." Neil L. Andersen

"The unseen God is at work in the darkness, in the doubts, in the disappointments, and in the delays." Alistair Begg

In Your Words

How much time each day do you enter the spiritual realm through prayer, meditation on the Word?

When you spend time with the Lord, do you see the world around you in a different way? Describe how.

Have you ever had "God moments" in your life that have transformed you? What were the experiences and how were you transformed?

In Your Journal

Say It. Pray It Share it.

Holy Spirit, help me see with eyes of faith and experience the unseen, the spiritual realities through which the Lord, my God, guides me, protects me, and blesses me.

God Shines Through Dirty Windows

In My Words

A day after I had not had one of my better days as a Christian, I received a phone call. It was a friend of mine telling me her brother was in the hospital and had just been hooked up to a breathing machine. She said he had complained about stomach pains, had pneumonia, and was not doing well.

Before leaving for the hospital, I began thinking about how my friend began her conversation. She mentioned a prayer I posted on Facebook the previous day and said she had to call me and ask for prayer. My prayer was for anyone who was hospitalized. I prayed the Holy Spirit would enter the halls and rooms of hospitals and protect those about to receive treatment, and the families and friends who waited for news.

I was not worthy to be used by God, and he agreed.

I sat in my car second guessing myself. "Gary, you are not worthy to minister to your friend." The previous day was not one of my better days as a Christian. In fact, instead of walking the Christian walk, I stumbled and fumbled, and then fell. I certainly was not worthy to be used by the Lord.

That's when the Lord stepped in. He agreed with me, but reminded me that he shines through dirty windows, a fact I've point out to my life coaching clients.

Driving home after my visit, I was struck by how the Lord used me, how he aligned everything to use me, despite my being a dirty window. I recalled the prayer I posted earlier that day. I prayed about how the Lord asks us to be lights on a hill, how his light vanishes darkness. I asked him to use me to bring comfort to someone who needed his loving touch.

One of the most memorable marketing themes was used by Windex claiming its window cleaner did its job so well the glass seemed to disappear. This is the same way we need to approach answering the Lord's call for us to serve others. When the Lord asks us to serve, we should respond in a way that glorifies him, not ourselves. As his light shines through windows like you and me, and dirty windows at that, we should disappear, allowing his love, mercy, and grace to shine through.

In God's Words

All of us have become like one who is unclean, and all our righteous acts are like filthy rags; we all shrivel up like a leaf, and like the wind our sins sweep us away. (Isaiah 64:6)

By myself I can do nothing; I judge only as I hear, and my judgment is just, for I seek not to please myself but him who sent me. (John 5:30)

For we do not have a high priest who is unable to empathize with our weaknesses, but we have one who has been tempted in every way, just as we are—yet he did not sin. (Hebrews 4:15)

Also read: John 5:19-20, Romans 3:23, Galatians 5:16

In the Words of Others

"Let us consider ourselves unworthy of being used by God and having others think of us, and then we will be well off." St. Vincent de Paul

"We are more sinful and flawed in ourselves than we ever dared to believe, yet at the very same time we are more loved and accepted in Jesus Christ than we ever dared hope." Timothy Keller

"There is something perfect to be found in the imperfect: the law keeps balance through the juxtaposition of beauty, which gains perfection through nurtured imperfection." Dejan Stojanovic

In Your Words

Have you felt the Lord leading you to do something but delayed because you felt unworthy? Recall the circumstances.

How has the Lord used you to serve others in ways you never thought were possible? Describe the circumstances and how you believe the Lord was involved.

Recall an instance when you felt emotionally or mentally unprepared to do something, and you turned to the Lord in prayer. What happened?

In Your Journal

Say It. Pray It. Share It.

My Lord and my God, as I go about serving you, may I always remember to give you all the honor and glory. May I remember to decrease as you increase when I serve others.

God Walked the Factory Floor

In My Words

The Total Quality Management (TQM) movement that emerged in the 1980s has been reinventing itself as the business and management landscape changes. One of its key principles is the importance of owners and managers "walking the floor," getting out of their offices and seeing what's really happening on the front line of their businesses.

A more visible example is the TV show, *Undercover Boss*, a show featuring owners, presidents, and CEOs of companies who are disguised to go undercover to discover how their employees do their jobs and represent the company.

Little did the original TQM gurus know the original floor walker was God himself. Walking the floor is exactly what God did after creating the world. After he rested and expressed satisfaction with what he created, he walked in the garden, paying attention to what was really going on. He even made an executive decision and fired his only two employees.

Jesus walked the factory floor for 33 years.

Thousands of years later, he turned his business over to his Son, Jesus Christ. Jesus walked the floor for 33 years, and completely revolutionized the business, rewriting the rules, hiring new employees, and totally revamping the corporate culture.

Before the Son moved on to his new position seated at the right hand of the founding Father, he passed the baton to us in a small room where the Holy Spirit came on board as a consultant to guide us, strengthen us, and walk alongside us as we walked the floors of our own individual franchises operating in the Kingdom of God here on earth.

As Christians, we have been charged with running our own little franchises, taking care of the Lord's business here on earth. We paid no franchise fee. Jesus paid that fee when he died on the cross for us. And there's no maintenance fee. He is always at our side ready to provide us his mercy and grace.

The Holy Spirit is present in us as the "helper" Jesus assigned to give us guidance, strength, and the marketing support we need through his power and the Word. And unlike many original founders who pass businesses to later generations, the Father is eternally alive and present, always available to communicate with us about how we are managing.

If you know of anyone interested in a business that is guaranteed to succeed, pass along the Good News about this great opportunity.

In God's Words

Whatever you do, work at it with all your heart, as working for the Lord, not for human masters, since you know that you will receive an inheritance from the Lord as a reward. It is the Lord Christ you are serving. (Colossians 3:23-24)

Let us not become weary in doing good, for at the proper time we will reap a harvest if we do not give up. Therefore, as we have opportunity, let us do good to all people, especially to those who belong to the family of believers. (Galatians 6:9-10)

This, then, is how you should pray: "Our Father in heaven, hallowed be your name, your kingdom come, your will be done, on earth as it is in heaven." (Matthew 6:9-10)

Also read: Genesis 2:15, Proverbs 13:4, Romans 14:17

In the Words of Others

"Pray as if everything depended on God. Work as if everything depended on you." St. Augustine

"The one supreme business of life is to find God's plan for your life and live it." E. Stanley Jones

"We are not here to build our empire only but also to help people discern the Kingdom of God." Sunday Adelaja

In Your Words

Describe what you consider to be the Lord's business here on earth based on the Old Testament. In the gospels?

How do you believe you have been called to walk the floor and help build the Kingdom of God here on earth?

Create a mission statement for your individual franchise of the Lord's business here on earth. Read it every day.

In Your Journal

Say It. Pray It. Share It.

Father God, you passed on to me a great responsibility, to bring people to you and to help establish your kingdom here on earth. Help me to succeed and glorify you.

Are You a Force to Be Reckoned With?

In My Words

The scriptures are clear. Jesus Christ was a force to be reckoned with from the time he was born to his ascension into heaven. But how?

Christ could have called his angels down to lift him up if he threw himself down from the highest point of the temple, as Satan suggested in the desert, but he didn't. The chief priests, elders, and scribes mocked him and said if he was King of Israel, he should come down from the cross. They said they would then believe in him. Surely, he could have summoned his angels to himself at the cross, but he didn't. And God the Father could bring his judgement and wrath down on you and me daily as he did throughout the Old Testament, but he doesn't.

You would think Jesus, as the Son of God and God in the flesh, would have demonstrated unbelievable force and power, but he didn't. As he walked this earth, the Lord seemed to do the exact opposite. He was not the powerful king and savior the Jews expected, and he certainly didn't have much influence, at least not with the "powers to be" at the time. Yet ultimately, he was a force to reckoned with, a force of peace, love, and hope that changed the world.

Jesus Christ came as a force to be reckoned with.

A force to be reckoned with is someone who is strong and cannot be ignored, someone who is up and coming, and whose power and influence must be considered. Tiger Woods was considered to be a force to be reckoned with on the PGA Tour as observers saw things in the young player beyond his years.

In a similar way, Jesus as a child astounded the rabbis in the synagogue with his wisdom and knowledge of the scriptures. When he grew older, he quietly and humbly went about preaching, healing, and serving.

One of the underlying themes of the life of Jesus is the way he related to ordinary people and his critics, who would soon become his enemies. He certainly could have become a "wrecking ball," wreaking the wrath and power of God on those who opposed him. The cleansing of the temple in righteous anger aside, Jesus came to this earth and left it in humility, not leaving behind a path of hatred and retribution, but a road paved with goodness, wisdom, love, and service.

This is the Jesus who shows us how to be a force to be reckoned with in our lives. His influence grew due to his message and his living out that message, not by force or manipulating people for personal gain. We too can be a force to be reckoned in the same way as we live the Gospel of Jesus Christ, as we live in goodness, wisdom, love, and service.

In God's Words

For to be sure, he was crucified in weakness, yet he lives by God's power. Likewise, we are weak in him, yet by God's power we will live with him in our dealing with you. (2 Corinthians 13:4)

For the Spirit God gave us does not make us timid, but gives us power, love and self-discipline. (2 Timothy 1:7)

You, God, are awesome in your sanctuary; the God of Israel gives power and strength to his people. Praise be to God! (Psalm 68:35)

Also read: Isaiah 40:29-31, 2 Corinthians 12:9, Ephesians 3:20

In the Words of Others

"Being powerful is like being a lady. If you have to tell people you are, you aren't." Margaret Thatcher

"The measure of a man is what he does with power." Plato

"Nearly all men can stand adversity, but if you want to test a man's character, give him power." Abraham Lincoln

In Your Words

What are the ways you believe a person could be a person to be reckoned with or a wrecking ball in a physical, emotional, intellectual, or spiritual way?

Have you ever been in a position of power and influence in your work and career? Were you a positive force or a negative influence at the time?

Cite examples of how you were in a position of power and influence in your family or social situations, and how you could have been a "wrecking ball," and not a positive force.

In Your Journal

Say It. Pray It. Share It.

Holy Spirit, help me discern at all times how I can be a positive force in my life and relationships as opposed to a negative influence. May I live a life of love and service.

Are You Managing Your God-Given Assets?

In My Words

Are you a good asset manager of the talents, learned skills, and experiences God gave you? Have you identified the spiritual gifts God has given you through the Holy Spirit?

The scripture most often quoted about how we handle our God-given assets is the Parable of the Talents found in Matthew's Gospel. The servant who didn't properly use the talents given him was called a worthless servant to be cast into the outer darkness.

The Lord leaves no doubt he wants us to use the personal assets he has given us. And he makes it crystal clear, properly using our personal assets will help us fulfill our God-given purpose and bring great benefits to us and others.

You need to deploy, operate, maintain, and upgrade.

Asset management refers to anything done to monitor and maintain things of value. The term is most often used when talking about financial holdings, buildings, and intangible assets. In this context, how well your assets are managed depends on how well your assets are deployed, operating, maintained, and upgraded.

Determining how well you manage your God-given assets is a simple three-step process. First, take inventory of your assets, your abilities, learned skills, significant life experiences, and gifts of the Holy Spirit. Next, look at how you have deployed these assets over the years and how you might better do so in the future. Determine if you maximized what you were capable of doing. Finally, explore the ways you have pursued education and other opportunities to maintain and improve the skills God allowed you to acquire.

Once you complete your asset management review, you should do what every good manager does, design a plan to improve.

Identify the way you can use, maintain, maximize, and continually upgrade your assets, especially your spiritual assets. One of the best ways to make sure you are making the most of your God-given assets is to practice the spiritual disciplines, including meditation, prayer, fasting, study, simplicity, submission, service, confession, and worship.

The spiritual disciplines are not legalistic rules, but tools to bring you closer to God. While adherence to the disciplines is not necessary for salvation, they should be a central part of helping you manage your God-given assets in your Christian walk.

In God's Words

We have different gifts, according to the grace given to each of us. If your gift is prophesying, then prophesy in accordance with your faith; (Romans 12:6-8)

And we know that in all things God works for the good of those who love him, who have been called according to his purpose. (Romans 8:28)

Have nothing to do with godless myths and old wives' tales; rather, train yourself to be godly. For physical training is of some value, but godliness has value for all things, holding promise for both the present life and the life to come. (1 Timothy 4:7-8)

Also read: Psalm 119:97, Psalm 119:11, 2 Timothy 1:7

In the Words of Others

"When I stand before God at the end of my life, I would hope that I would not have a single bit of talent left, and could say, 'I used everything you gave me.'" Erma Bombeck

"Our talents are the gift that God gives to us...What we make of our talents is our gift back to God."
Leo F. Buscaglia

"Time and health are two precious assets that we don't recognize and appreciate until they have been depleted." Denis Waitley

"A person's most useful asset is not the head full of knowledge, but a heart full of love, an ear ready to listen, and a hand willing to help." Anonymous

In Your Words

Identify God-given assets that most influenced your personal or professional life. What do you think the Lord is telling you about your life purpose and his calling for you?

Read Romans 12:6-8 and 1 Corinthians 12:4-6. Prayerfully consider what gifts of the Spirit you may have received and the fruits they've born in your life.

Describe how you have deployed your God-given assets. Have you used them or ignored them? Consider ways you could improve.

In Your Journal

Say It. Pray It. Share It.

Father God, you blessed me with abilities, strengths, and spiritual gifts. You gave me opportunities to learn skills and benefit from life experiences. Help me use them to glorify you and serve others.

Perfection: The Impossible Dream

In My Words

There are people who get up in the morning and set out on a quest to be perfect in all they say and do, seeing their foibles and faults as giants to be conquered, when they are only simple windmills on life's landscape. They are like Don Quixote seeking perfection in an imperfect world.

In *Don Quixote,* the novel written by Miguel de Cervantes Saavedra, a nobleman by named Alonso Quixano loses his sanity as he reads novels about chivalry, a way of life he believes is lost. With a peasant farmer named Sancho Panza, he sets out to revive the world of chivalry and bring justice to the world under the name of Don Quixote de la Mancha.

Don Quixote imagines he is living out a story of a chivalrous knight undoing wrongs. His well-intentioned exploits create problems for himself and the characters he meets along the way. He eventually returns to his home village after experiencing defeat.

Is perfection available to you here on this earth?

Seeking to be perfect in what you do or say is an admirable goal. However, a person exhibiting perfectionism seeks to be flawless in all they do. They also hold themselves and others up to unreasonably high standards, and are critical with themselves and others when they fall short of those standards.

Pursuing the goal of perfection is a positive thing, but when it becomes perfectionism, it can get you into trouble, just as Don Quioxte's imaginings caused problems. In addition to putting excessive pressure on yourself, there are other signs you are on the wrong side of the pursuit of perfection.

You will never feel good enough or completely satisfied with anything you do. You are often excessively critical of yourself and others, unconsciously hiding your own imperfections. For you, everything is either good or bad. There is no middle ground. And you link your identity and worth to being perfect.

A healthier approach emphasizes being the very best you can be, more focused on the process of being who you are rather than what you accomplish or fail to do. As you strive daily to use your God-given abilities and gifts the way for which God purposed them, you are doing your very best to live the perfect life as the perfect you, as God envisioned for you.

Is there perfection available to you while you are on this earth? It is only when you have the love of God in you by following his Word that you are perfected, spiritually perfected, as you serve the way Jesus Christ served, not in an imaginary perfect way, but in the valleys serving others where life is real.

In God's Words

Indeed, there is no one on earth who is righteous, no one who does what is right and never sins. (Ecclesiastes 7:20)

Let perseverance finish its work so that you may be mature and complete, not lacking anything. (James 1:4)

Each of you should use whatever gift you have received to serve others, as faithful stewards of God's grace in its various forms. (1 Peter 4:10)

Also read: Deuteronomy 15:11, Philippians 3:12-14

In the Words of Others

"Perfectionism is a dangerous state of mind in an imperfect world." Robert Hillyer

"Seeking perfection in human affairs is a perfect way to destroy them." Jaron Lanier

"Perfectionism is self-abuse of the highest order."
Anne Wilson Schaef

In Your Words

Do you ever feel dissatisfied with everything you do? Do you feel unworthy when you fail to accomplish something?

Can you recall a time when your excessive criticism and unreasonably high expectations hurt a loved one or a friend? What could you have done differently?

What are the ways in which you can be more perfected here on earth by showing your love for God through serving others?

In Your Journal

Say It. Pray It, Share It.

Lord Jesus, help me remember perfection is only available through having and expressing your love, not my efforts to be flawless in all I say and do.

The Mind Is Connected to the Happy Bone

In My Words

Bobby McFerrin, an American jazz vocalist and conductor, climbed to the top of the charts in 1988 with his No. 1 pop hit, *Don't Worry, Be Happy*. McFerrin's inspiration for the song came from that exact saying often used by the Indian mystic and sage, Meher Baba. In an interview that year, McFerrin said the saying was a "pretty neat philosophy in four words."

The apostle Paul also expressed a pretty neat philosophy in Romans 12:2 when he wrote, "Do not conform to the pattern of this world but be transformed by the renewing of your mind. Then you will be able to test and approve what God's will is—his good, pleasing and perfect will."

Think positive and make your own sunshine!

It has been shown through scientific research and personal observation that there is a link between the mind and the body. If you hold on to negative thoughts like worry, anger, unforgiveness, and ill will towards others, these could be a potential cause, or at least contributing factors of illness. Hence the saying, being "worried sick."

Obviously, there is no such thing as a happy bone, but positive affirmations and prayer can bring about a desired state of being in oneself in which the mental, emotional, and physical state of the person changes for the better. With this in mind, I often tell people to make their own sunshine.

Take time in the morning to relax your body and breathe in the new day. Take some time to think about what makes you happy and things you like to do. Dwell on positive memories. Praise the Lord and thank him for another day full of opportunities to serve him and experience his love.

If negative thoughts arise, let them go and don't dwell on them. Just like positive thoughts, one negative thought leads to another. Avoid the noise created by television, radio, and social media, unless you make selections that relax and raise you up.

If you have a rain cloud over your head like Charlie Brown has sometimes, think positive and make your own sunshine through prayer and the Lord's presence. You'll be a bright ray of sunshine to those around you and feel a whole lot better mentally, emotionally, physically, and spiritually as you do the Lord's will.

In God's Words

You make known to me the path of life; you will fill me with joy in your presence, with eternal pleasures at your right hand. (Psalm 16:11)

But those who hope in the LORD will renew their strength. They will soar on wings like eagles; they will run and not grow weary, they will walk and not be faint. (Isaiah 40:31)

Rejoice always, pray continually, give thanks in all circumstances; for this is God's will for you in Christ Jesus. (1 Thessalonians 5:16-18)

Also read: Psalm 37:4, John 16:22, Philippians 4:7-8

In the Words of Others

"While other world views lead us to sit in the midst of life's joys, foreseeing the coming sorrows, Christianity empowers its people to sit in the midst of the world's sorrow, tasting the coming joy." Timothy Keller

"For every minute you are angry, you lose sixty seconds of happiness." Ralph Waldo Emerson

"Folks are usually about as happy as they make their minds up to be." Abraham Lincoln

"Happiness is when what you think, what you say, and what you do are in harmony." Mahatma Gandhi

In Your Words

Think of a day when you started the day with negative thoughts. How did it affect the rest of your day?

Can you think of a time when you were "worried sick?" If so, describe how you felt and how it affected your day.

Recall a time when you transformed a negative mood into a positive mood, or faced unexpected and challenging circumstances using positive affirmations or prayer.

In Your Journal

Say It. Pray It. Share It.

Lord Jesus, help me keep prayerfully positive in my daily life no matter what happens. Holy Spirit, help me commune daily with the mind of God so I can discern his holy and true will.

What's Your EQ?

In My Words

If you ask any person on the street about their IQ, you'll probably get a thoughtful look as he or she tries to remember what someone in their school days may have told them about their IQ, their intelligence quotient. If you ask the same person about their EI or EQ, chances are you'll get a blank "say what" stare.

Emotional Intelligence (EI), also known as Emotional Quotient (EQ), has been one of the darling concepts in the popular psychology community since Daniel Goleman published a book by that name.[3] However, despite the concept's popularity in the popular press, the scientific community has been critical of its validity, questioning the scientific basis for all the claims regarding its usefulness in explaining positive outcomes in social interactions and relationships.

Become better at controlling all your emotions.

In recent years, there has been a growing body of thinking and evidence regarding the lasting neurological effects of emotions and the role they play in how we think. Without "getting into the weeds," as the saying goes, regarding the scientific validity of the connection between thinking and emotions, there are ways knowing how to recognize your emotions and those of others, that can help you in your personal growth, professional advancement, and being more effective in your Christian walk.

When you interact with others, the ability to immediately recognize the other person's emotions is an important part of processing information about the person and how to react to them. As you become more aware of your own emotions and your ability to perceive those of others, you can manage the interaction using emotions, even negative ones, to achieve your goals. You can also become better at controlling your emotions, especially disruptive emotions, as you react to others and circumstances.

Being more aware of your own emotions and your ability to perceive those of other's can be beneficial for both children and adults. This awareness will help you have positive social interactions and relationships. The ability to know your emotions and manage them is also correlated with higher personal satisfaction, personal security, and how others perceive you as more pleasant, more agreeable, more empathetic.

All of the above benefits of controlling your emotions and reacting appropriately to those of others can be a significant help in your Christian walk as you witness to others through your words and actions.

In God's Words

Better a patient person than a warrior, one with self-control than one who takes a city. (Proverbs 16:32)

Fools show their annoyance at once, but the prudent overlook an insult. (Proverbs 12:16)

In your anger do not sin: Do not let the sun go down while you are still angry, and do not give the devil a foothold. (Ephesians 4:26-27)

Also read: Proverbs 25:28, 1 Corinthians 13:1-13, Galatians 5:22-23

In the Words of Others

"Take control of your consistent emotions and begin to consciously and deliberately reshape your daily experience of us." Tony Robbins

"One ought to hold on to one's heart; for if one lets it go, one soon loses control of the head too." Friedrich Nietzsche

In Your Words

Rate yourself 1-10 on how good you are in recognizing your own emotions in social interactions and relationships. Why?

Rate yourself 1-10 on how well you appropriately respond to others' emotions, especially in challenging situations. Why?

Cite instances when your ability to recognize another's emotions helped you in your Christian walk.

In Your Journal

Say It. Pray It. Share It.

Holy Spirit, give me special insight into how I can recognize the emotions of others, and best respond to them in an appropriate and loving way, even when anger may feel like the best response.

Playing Hide-and-Seek with Yourself

In My Words

One of my favorite childhood games was Hide-and-Seek. I'm not sure why it was my favorite because I was usually the first one caught and had trouble finding the other kids. If you are one of the few who has been deprived of the opportunity to play Hide-and-Seek, here is a brief tutorial.

The game has been played by children for decades around the world in various forms. One player closes his or her eyes for a short period counting to 100, or whatever time players choose, while the other players hide. When time is up, the child who is the seeker opens his or her eyes and looks for the others. When the first hider is found, that child becomes the next seeker. Players often designate a "safe home base" they touch to offset the seeker's advances.

How do we play hide-and-seek with ourselves?

If you conducted a "man-on-the-street" interview, you would find few people who would admit to not knowing themselves very well. Our hubris tells us, "Sure, you know all about yourself." And no doubt, most of us do know a great deal about ourselves. However, there is a "safe home base" in each of us where we hide from ourselves as we try to neutralize discomfort and painful thoughts about ourselves.

How do we escape to this "safe home base?" We consciously or unconsciously take diversionary actions to deceive ourselves as we redirect our thinking and that of others, ignoring our faults and areas in which need to improve, and make changes to experience personal and professional growth and success.

For example, if someone is accusing us of something, we may shift blame to another person. Or, we might make excuses for our behavior. Another tactic often used is minimizing our behavior. We are even capable of combining all three as in this example.

"I was late for the meeting because the weather was bad and my wife forgot to set the alarm. Besides, is it really a big deal that I was late for the meeting?" These statements may be true, but the reality may also be that he rolled over and turned off the alarm, something he needs to address. If he keeps making excuses, shifting blame, and minimizing his behavior, there will eventually be negative consequences. Furthermore, he may be missing opportunities for personal improvement and professional growth.

We all play Hide-and-Seek with ourselves. But remember, God doesn't play by the same rules we do. He never closes his eyes and you have no place to hide from him.

In God's Words

For by the grace given me I say to every one of you: Do not think of yourself more highly than you ought, but rather think of yourself with sober judgment, in accordance with the faith God has distributed to each of you. (Romans 12:3)

I do not understand what I do. For what I want to do I do not do, but what I hate I do. And if I do what I do not want to do, I agree that the law is good. As it is, it is no longer I myself who do it, but it is sin living in me. For I know that good itself does not dwell in me, that is, in my sinful nature. For I have the desire to do what is good, but I cannot carry it out. For I do not do the good I want to do, but the evil I do not want to do—this I keep on doing. (Romans 7:15-19)

79

Also Read: Proverbs 19:8, Jeremiah 17:9, James 1:5

In the Words of Others

"If most of us remain ignorant of ourselves, it is because self-knowledge is painful and we prefer the pleasures of illusion." Aldous Huxley

"Knowledge of self is the mother of all knowledge. So, it is incumbent on me to know myself, to know it completely, to know its minutiae, its characteristics, its subtleties and its very atoms." Kahlil Gibran

In Your Words

List five positives about you. Consider your God-given abilities and learned skills. Then list five negative qualities.

List things you might not know or want to know about yourself. Dig deep to explore your "safe home base."

Describe ways you may have consciously or unconsciously deceived yourself about your faults or areas in which you need improvement. How will you make the needed changes?

In Your Journal

Say it. Pray it. Share it.

My Lord and my God, you are the light that came into this world to banish darkness. I ask that you shine a light into my heart and soul to help me see myself as I truly am.

Worrying About Being a Worry Wart

In My Words

In the early 1920s, cartoonist J.R. Williams included a character called Worry Wart in his comic strip *Out our Way*, panels based on amusing situations and his own life experiences. Initially, the Worry Wart character caused other characters in the comic strip to worry. As time went on, the meaning of the name came to mean the opposite. It came to mean a person who worries excessively about things.

If you worry, there's good news and bad news. The good news is worry has its benefits. Worry can motivate you to act, to accomplish things you might have put off, and to face problems head on and solve them. Worry can make you more alert to details and help you avoid surprises.

Worry distracts you and drains your energy.

Then there's the bad news. Worry can disrupt your daily life as you dwell on what could happen and not pay attention to what God is doing in your life and expecting from you. Worry distracts you and drains your energy. It is a waste of time and can even paralyze you. And isn't it interesting that at some point you end up worrying about how much you worry.

We often dwell on things such as difficulties and troubles even though there is no apparent reason to do so. Have you found that most of the things you worry about never happen?

Here is an activity you can use to help you cure yourself of the worry wart mentality. Make sure you first prayerfully make God part of the process, asking him to be a lamp until your feet and a light unto your path.

Take a plain sheet of paper. Designate the first column "Worries." This is the column in which you list the things about which you worry. Keep it simple. Use a word or short phrase. List whatever comes to mind.

In the second column, list worries in the first you cannot affect. In the third column, list the worries in the first about which you can do something. In the fourth column, note things about which you worry that could fall into columns two or three. These could be things over which you have some but not complete control. Put the sheet of paper away and revisit it.

In God's Words

Do not be anxious about anything, but in every situation, by prayer and petition, with thanksgiving, present your requests to God. And the peace of God, which transcends all understanding, will guard your hearts and your minds in Christ Jesus. (Philippians 4:6-7)

Therefore, do not worry about tomorrow, for tomorrow will worry about itself. Each day has enough trouble of its own. (Matthew 6:34)

Also read: Matthew 11:28-30, Proverbs 12:25, John 14:1

In the Words of Others

"I am an old man and have known a great many troubles, but most of them have never happened." Mark Twain

"Do not anticipate trouble or worry about what may never happen. Keep in the sunlight." Benjamin Franklin

"Sorrow looks back, Worry looks around, Faith looks up." Ralph Waldo Emerson

In Your Words

Revisit your list occasionally. Ask yourself the following:

Why did I place the worries in column two, three, or four?

What surprises me about my choices?

Which "mole-hill worries" have I made into mountains?

Which items are actionable?

Create a plan of action and make a commitment to follow through. Make God part of the process through prayer and meditating on his Word. You will see that much of your worrying is a needless waste of your time and energy, time and energy that could be dedicated to serving the Lord and others.

In Your Journal

Say It. Pray It. Share It.

Lord Jesus, I place all my worries in your hands, for only you have absolute control over the future. I realize each time I dwell on a worry, I am distracted from focusing on you and what you want me to accomplish.

How to Tame an Elephant in Your Life

In My Words

No doubt you've heard the saying about the elephant in the room, the issue, situation, or problem no one wants to talk about or deal with, but the one everyone knows is there, an anxious pachyderm lurking in the back of everyone's mind, waiting to burst out of the bushes into the open.

Is there an elephant in your life? Is there an issue, situation, or problem you don't want to deal with, or you're are afraid of facing, but know it's there and needs your attention?

The elephant in your life could be a belly that keeps growing due to poor eating habits, or a pain in the side you keep ignoring. It could be an addiction you'll deal with tomorrow. It could be a sin behavior that you have convinced yourself is no big deal every time you give in to temptation.

Baby elephants like Dumbo, the junior elephant with big ears in the Disney film by that name, are cute and harmless. But when you ignore the impatient pachyderm in your life that needs attention, it grows larger and larger until you have to deal with it immediately or suffer the consequences.

It's time to send the pachyderm in your life packing.

Whether you have one elephant in your life or a herd, it's time to act. It's time to tame the elephant in your life, grab it by the trunk, and send the pachyderm packing. You do this by confronting the floppy-eared pachyderm. You may have ignored it for a long time, but plant your feet mentally and emotionally on the ground and look the issue, situation, or problem in the eyes.

A good next step is to realize you are not the only one facing the long-eared mammal you have been consciously or unconsciously ignoring. If you look around in life's jungle, you'll see others struggling to tame the same wild beast.

Next, you need to assess what will happen because you have ignored the pesky pachyderm, and then take action. What action should you take? That depends on whether the elephant is moseying around and the issue is not critical, or it begins charging and needs immediate action. Even national park and wildlife experts disagree on exactly what to do when the largest and most impressive beast in the jungle begins to attack in the brush or on a savannah.

There are many experts who can help you take corrective action. But remember, God is also faithfully standing beside you as he said he would, regardless of how huge the elephant or herd may be. All you have to do is take his powerful right hand and stand your ground in prayer.

In God's Words

No temptation has overtaken you except what is common to mankind. And God is faithful; he will not let you be tempted beyond what you can bear. But when you are tempted, he will also provide a way out so that you can endure it. (1 Corinthians 10:13)

Cast your cares on the LORD and he will sustain you; he will never let the righteous be shaken. (Psalm 55:22)

Therefore, since we have these promises, dear friends, let us purify ourselves from everything that contaminates body and spirit, perfecting holiness out of reverence for God. (2 Corinthians 7:1)

Also Read: 1 Samuel 17:45, 2 Corinthians 4:8-9, James 1:2-4

In the Words of Others

"Sometimes you don't realize your own strength until you come face to face with your greatest weakness."
Susan Gayle

"Love will draw an elephant through a key-hole."
Samuel Richardson

"Don't just run from temptation, look it in the eye and defeat it." Baylor Barbee

In Your Words

What is the elephant in your life you have been ignoring? Do you have more than one trumpeting for your attention?

What are the consequences of not taming the elephant? Have you pictured your life if you let the elephant run amuck?

Imagine focusing on what life would be without the elephant in your life? How does this make you feel?

In Your Journal

Say It. Pray It. Share It.

My Lord and my God, I come before you and ask you to help me overcome _____. Please continue to walk by my side and pick me up when I stumble and backslide.

Humility: Not Eating Humble Pie

In My Words

In his best-selling book, *The Purpose Driven Life: What on Earth Am I Here for?* Pastor Rick Warren suggests "humility is not putting yourself down or denying your strengths; rather, it is being honest about your weaknesses."[4] This profound statement flies in the face of the way most of us would define humility.

When someone is forced to "eat humble pie," as the saying goes, we say they are admitting they have done something wrong and are apologizing. The derivation of the word 'humble' comes from old Latin and French words for loins, leading to it being associated with something unpleasant and humiliating. The old word 'umbl' referred to the inner parts of a deer. The story goes that when rich people enjoyed the better parts of the deer, their servants ate the 'umbles' which were baked into a pie. Hence the subservient meaning of the phrase and why humility often gets a bad rap.

True humility is being honest about our weaknesses, but it is also not thinking of less of ourselves because of our weaknesses. It is a state of mind directed outward, away from ourselves. This, of course, begs the question, if we are to think of ourselves less, of what should we think about more? I suggest three answers: God, others, and yes, ourselves.

Humility is a way of life we should adopt and live.

The outward trajectory of humility should be directed toward God and others. We are humble before God as fallen creatures. And even as Christians who have been saved as children of God and destined for eternal life with the Lord, we remain humble and meek before God as his servants.

In a complementary way, as God's servants, we are to serve others, thinking of ourselves less as we give of our time and other resources to help God's people, all his people. We should decrease so others might increase, as John the Baptist did for Jesus.

Humility should also include thinking more about ourselves as deliberately being outward oriented towards God and others, not running on automatic. Humility should be a way of life we intentionally adopt and live as much possible minute by minute, hour by hour, day by day, until we die. It is not just a state of mind, it is a state of life we need to develop as we recognize our insufficiency before God and his call to serve others using our God-given gifts.

The caveat to this is while we intentionally seek to live a humble way of life, this should not be a way lined with extreme self-denial, or pride in being virtuous.

Persons who maintain a true humble lifestyle are not arrogant or boastful. They are teachable, ready to learn from others. Most importantly, they are ready to give of themselves in service. They are deliberately mindful of their part in God's plan as they serve with a lowly spirit in the face of God's overwhelming love for them.

In God's Words

For all those who exalt themselves will be humbled, and those who humble themselves will be exalted. (Luke 14:11)

Pride brings a person low, but the lowly in spirit gain honor. (Proverbs 29:23)

Finally, all of you, be like-minded, be sympathetic, love one another, be compassionate and humble. (1 Peter 3:8)

Also read: James 4:6, Philippians 2:3-11, 2 Chronicles 7:14

In the Words of Others

"As long as you are proud you cannot know God. A proud man is always looking down on things and people: and, of course, as long as you are looking down you cannot see something that is above you." C.S. Lewis

"True humility does not know that it is humble. If it did, it would be proud from the contemplation of so fine a virtue." Martin Luther

In Your Words

Does your understanding of true humility match what you just read above?

If your understanding of humility is different from the above, describe your understanding of humility.

Have you met people who demonstrate the type of true humility described above? Describe why you think so.

In Your Journal

Say It. Pray It. Share It.

Lord Jesus, help me live a life of humility, recognizing my insufficiency before you and my need to decrease so those I love and serve can increase.

Time to Empty Your Shopping Bag

In My Words

A Roman Catholic priest was well-known in my neighborhood for his "shopping bag sermons." He would leave the sanctuary and stand before the congregation holding a shopping bag. The congregation, especially those in the front pews, would anxiously wait for him to open his bag and begin his sermon, dipping into his bag for his props.

Many years later, I borrowed the idea and used it during my ministries at nursing homes and in life coaching sessions to demonstrate the effects of guilt and how to address them.

I would load a shopping bag with canned fruit, canned vegetables, sloppy joe mix in cans, tuna in cans, and whatever else I could find in my kitchen. My only requirement was weight. The shopping bag had to test my arm strength when I lifted it.

During my ministry or life coaching sessions, I would drop the bag in front of my audience or client with a thud. I unloaded the bag one can at a time, calling each an unresolved feeling of guilt until the bag was empty. I then waved the empty bag in the air like a magician who just made his beautiful assistant disappear.

Unresolved guilt is a heavy burden to carry around.

Guilt is an indication of emotional distress. It can be a valuable emotion if dealt with in a timely manner. It can bring a person to make amends with someone he or she offended, and even to do something good as a result. But unresolved guilt is a heavy burden that weighs us down, and unlike canned food items, it is far from being healthy for us if held for long and not addressed appropriately.

Guilt becomes inappropriate and damaging when the person who committed the offense internalizes that he or she did something wrong and begins to identify themselves by the behavior. The person with "bad behavior" is transformed into a "bad person."

Guilt becomes a destructive burden when it negatively affects your behavior. If you perceive yourself as a "bad person," you begin to question what you do and the decisions you make, and you're more prone to misinterpret events as your responsibility. You may also feel guilty about doing things that you enjoy and may be healthy for you.

You can begin emptying that shopping bag of guilt by accepting guilt as a good emotion and be thankful that you were reminded of what to do and not to do. But then move on to resolve your guilt.

Apologize to someone if necessary and forgive yourself, acknowledging that you are a good person who just did something wrong, and that God has already forgiven you. Begin by putting positive things in your bag, prayer, positive affirmations, and the Lord's peace.

Turn to God throughout your process of healing, especially if you disobey one of his commands through sin. As when seeking the forgiveness of a friend you wronged, confess your wrongdoing to God, repent, and be thankful for his mercy and grace. Be ready to forgive others as he forgave you.

In God's Words

Let the wicked forsake their ways and the unrighteous their thoughts. Let them turn to the LORD, and he will have mercy on them, and to our God, for he will freely pardon. (Isaiah 55:7)

My guilt has overwhelmed me like a burden too heavy to bear. (Psalm 38:4)

Godly sorrow brings repentance that leads to salvation and leaves no regret, but worldly sorrow brings death. (2 Corinthians 7:10)

Also read: Micah 7:18-19, Psalm 30:5, 1 John 1:9

In the Words of Others

"Guilt is the source of sorrows, the avenger fiend that follows us behind with whips and stings." Nicholas Rowe

"The difference between shame and guilt is the difference between 'I am bad' and 'I did something bad.'" Dr. Brene Brown

"Guilt is perhaps the most painful companion of death." Coco Chanel

In Your Words

Recall a time when you did something bad or behaved in a way that hurt someone. How quickly did you address the guilt?

Do you still feel guilty for something? If yes, how has this guilt affected your life? How you relate to the person you wronged?

Did you at any time feel that what you did made you a bad person? If yes, describe the feelings and why.

Do you believe God has ever played a role in how you handled your guilt about offending others? Elaborate on how, if yes.

In Your Journal

Say It. Pray It. Share It

Lord Jesus, help me remember you went to the cross for me, and no matter what I do, forgiveness awaits me if I repent. Cleanse me of guilt that keeps me from experiencing your love.

How to Ignore the Voice of Shame

In My Words

In 1945, Spade Cooley and the Western Swing Dance Gang played *Shame on You*, the first in a series of six top ten singles for the group. The song tells the story of a fellow confronting his girlfriend who is running around with other guys. The song's lyrics, especially the final lyrics, tell us all we need to know about how shame affects us and how we interact with others because of it.

The lyrics unapologetically describe the effects of shame, including not being able to hold one's head up high, and being unable to look others in the eye. The song is a powerful reminder of what shame can do to us.

Shame is a natural emotion we experience when we have done something wrong or embarrassing. As opposed to guilt which pertains to what we have done, shame refers to a painful and distressing internal feeling. When we feel shame, we think less of ourselves, prompting us to want to hide and not face others, literally and emotionally. Our whole demeanor changes. It's as though a weight is bearing down on us.

There is a more powerful voice than shame.

In the Book of Genesis, Adam and Eve disobeyed God and ate fruit from the Tree of Knowledge despite God's command not to do so. They disobeyed and disappointed the only friend in the world they had, their creator. They immediately had their eyes opened and became aware of their nakedness. They were exposed. They sewed fig leaves together and made coverings for themselves. When they heard God walking in the garden, they hid among the trees in the garden. They couldn't look their friend, their creator, in the eyes. They had shame.

94

This biblical account illustrates how we feel after doing something wrong or embarrassing, and how destructive shame can be. Can you imagine how they felt inside? Can you fathom the depths of their shame after disobeying their only friend in the world, with whom they had walked daily?

Shame has a voice. It tells us we're no good, inferior, and unworthy of respect. When we listen to it, we start down the proverbial rabbit's hole. If we continue to listen, our feelings can run the gamut of anger, despair, and even depression.

There is a more powerful voice, the voice of the Lord our God, the same voice that confronted, cursed, and banished Adam and Eve. However, while still capable of judgement, that voice now speaks to us with mercy and forgiveness.

Once we face and expose what has caused us shame, confess our sins, and accept his forgiveness, shame is neutralized. Even if our actions are not sins, but embarrassing actions we regret, the Lord is there to help us recognize our imperfection and move on with the help of the Holy Spirit.

Shame can play a role in convicting us of ways we fall short of our expectations, those of others, and God's. But through the power of the Holy Spirit, and being in God's Word to claim his promises and his truth, we can face feelings telling us we are unworthy of God's love and friendship of those around us.

In God's Words

Do not be afraid; you will not be put to shame. Do not fear disgrace; you will not be humiliated. You will forget the shame of your youth and remember no more the reproach of your widowhood. (Isaiah 54:4)

No temptation has overtaken you except what is common to mankind. And God is faithful; he will not let you be tempted beyond what you can bear. But when you are tempted, he will also provide a way out so that you can endure it. (1 Corinthians)

My little children, I am writing these things to you so that you may not sin. But if anyone does sin, we have an advocate with the Father, Jesus Christ the righteous. (1 John 2:1)

Also read: Micah 7:19, Psalm 40:11-12, Romans 3:23

In the Words of Others

"Shame arises from the fear of men, conscience from the fear of God." Samuel Johnson

"Shame is a soul-eating emotion." C. J. Jung

"God never leads the soul through guilt, shame, or fear, but attracts the soul through love." Richard Rohr

In Your Words

Recall a time when you felt shame or shamed by others. What feelings did you experience at the time?

In what ways did the feelings impact your life? In what ways did your reactions to shame impact others?

Has the Lord been involved in your experience of shame? If he was, describe your feelings at the time?

In Your Journal

Say It. Pray It. Share It.

Holy Spirit, renew my strength and attitude when I stumble so I can obediently do the Father's will. Release any shame I may experience when I fail to do so.

To Forgive or Wait for the Next Dance?

In My Words

Remember the days when you went to a high school dance and most of the guys stood against one wall with their hands in their pockets trying to muster up enough nerve to ask a girl to dance? They stood there looking at each other, up at the ceiling, or checking their watches. If a girl approached or someone encouraged them to dance, the common refrain was, "I'm waiting for the next dance." And that next dance usually never came.

I had a life coaching client tell me he couldn't understand why he was having so much trouble forgiving. We discovered together that his inability to forgive was poisoning a long-time friendship and was dominating his thinking. He told me he was waiting for his friend to say she was sorry for what she had done before he would forgive her. He said, "I'm ready to forgive Sally (not her real name) but I'm waiting for her to say she's sorry."

True forgiveness has no strings attached, no "buts."

I asked him to repeat what he just said and think about it. The "aha moment" came when he discovered he was linking something he could control to something over which he had no control. In his own way, he was standing against the wall at the dance with his hands in his pocket waiting for a girl to come and ask him to dance.

Forgiveness is a solo act before God. Reconciliation is a coming together. For reconciliation to occur, it takes two to tango, and often the dance partner is not ready to take the dance floor.

One of the reasons people can't bring themselves to forgive another person of a wrong done to them is that they are waiting for the offender to say they're sorry. They think reconciliation is the same as forgiveness, or feel reconciliation comes before forgiveness, when in fact forgiveness and reconciliation are not the same and forgiveness comes first.

True forgiveness has no strings attached. There are no "buts." If we add strings expecting an apology before forgiving, we are standing in judgement before the offender, requiring some type of payment. And there is only one who is qualified to judge, God the almighty. In fact, he sent his Son to the cross to atone for our sins, freely forgiving us with no strings attached.

In God's Words

Then Peter came to Jesus and asked, "Lord, how many times shall I forgive my brother or sister who sins against me? Up to seven times?" Jesus answered, "I tell you, not seven times, but seventy-seven times." (Matthew 18:21-22)

Bear with each other and forgive one another if any of you has a grievance against someone. Forgive as the Lord forgave you. (Colossians 3:13)

Hatred stirs up conflict, but love covers over all wrongs.
(Proverbs 10:12)

Also Read: Psalm 103:10-14, Matthew 6:14-15, Ephesians 4:32

In the Words of Others

"Life becomes easier when you learn to accept the apology you never got." Robert Brault

"Forgiveness is the giving up of resentment against someone. And our right to get even no matter what has been done to us." Dr. Charles F. Stanley

"Forgiveness is not an occasional act, it is a constant attitude." Martin Luther King Jr.

In Your Words

Are you having trouble forgiving someone? Describe what has to happen before you forgive the person or persons. Are you waiting for them to say they're sorry?

Have you been waiting for someone to forgive you? Describe why you think the person or persons have not forgiven you.

How do you feel about Christ's suggestion that you must forgive "not seven times, but seventy-seven times?"

In Your Journal

Share It. Pray It. Share It.

Lord Jesus, when I find it difficult to forgive someone, help me to remember how you went to the cross and died for me. Help me forgive without waiting for an apology.

Patiently Waiting for God's Downloads

In My Words

I sat at my desk one morning staring at the blue computer screen watching the twirling dots as my computer downloaded updates. Seconds passed. Minutes passed, and passed, and passed. 10%, 11%, 12%. As the percentages slowly climbed, my patience quickly declined.

"Come on, I have things to do," I told the computer. The computer didn't answer me. It just kept twirling those little white dots. I said to myself, "Be patient, just wait." So, I did. While I waited, I began praying. And as the update percentage reached 25%, I thought, "Maybe God has some updates for me."

Check your spiritual downloads daily for updates.

What a teachable moment! Was God telling me I should come before him in prayer and quiet time for his updates before I start each day? Was he telling me I need to be patient as he downloads what he wants to tell me, and not begin rushing into my day? Was it also a time when I can update him on my needs and the needs of others?

God is constantly talking to us. He longs for a close relationship with us. A long-standing bond between two close friends facilitates their ability to communicate with each other. An intimate relationship between a husband and wife creates the optimum scenario for mutual understanding, even in silent moments. In the same way, our ability to hear God and his message is in direct proportion to the closeness of our relationship with him.

The next time you're waiting for your computer to finish processing, or any time you have to wait at the doctor's office, airport, or on the phone, ask God if he has anything to tell you. Think about something you need to tell him. The Lord already knows your thoughts, but your asking is an expression of faith and shows your appreciation for his being in your life.

Make listening to God a priority. You must be ready to hear him and obey him. This will help increase your sensitivity to him. Also spend time in his Word. Other ways to increase your receptiveness are prayer, meditation, and worship. It's often much easier to talk to God than to listen to him. But if your heart and mind are open to his messages, you'll relish the time spent waiting for his daily updates, unlike watching twirling dots on your computer screen.

In God's Words

In the morning, LORD, you hear my voice; in the morning I lay my requests before you and wait expectantly.
(Psalm 5:3)

Call to me and I will answer you and tell you great a and unsearchable things you do not know. (Jeremiah 33:3)

My sheep listen to my voice; I know them, and they follow me. (John 10:27)

Also read: Proverbs 2:1-5, Job 33:14-15, John 8:47

In the Words of Others

"If we have listening ears, God speaks to us in our own language, whatever that language may be."
Mahatma Gandhi

"Listen in silence because if your heart is full of other things you cannot hear the voice of God." Mother Theresa

"Intimacy with God is not experienced through monolog prayers but through reflective listening as well as earnest petitioning." Gary Rohrmayer

In Your Words

When you pray in the morning, is your prayer experience interactive, allowing time and silence for the Lord to speak? If so, recall a time and how it affected your day.

When you receive a "download" from the Lord, do you spend time meditating on it and considering its significance for your daily Christian walk?

What can you do to make your time with the Lord more fruitful when receiving "downloads" from him?

What prevents you from taking the time to listen to the Lord's messages? What can you do to correct that?

In Your Journal

Say It. Pray It. Share It.

Lord Jesus, I pray I take the time every morning and throughout my day to listen to your voice. Holy Spirit, help me discern and follow the Father's holy and true will.

Having a Spirit of Thankfulness

In My Words

One of the more challenging passages found in the Bible is the scripture in 1 Thessalonians 5:16-18 that tells us to "give thanks in all circumstances." Notice the absolute nature of this scripture. There is no beating around the bush. There is no hedging of bets. If we try to live this scripture, we must be all in. Why? Because the second part of this scripture reads, "for this is God's will for you in Christ Jesus." God expects us to have an uncompromising attitude of gratitude.

It should also come as no surprise that having a spirit of thankfulness is good for your health and overall well-being. Research has shown that gratitude helps people feel more positive emotions, enjoy good experiences, improve their health and wellness, better handle problems that arise, and build strong relationships in all areas of their lives.

Gratitude helps people feel more positive emotions.

As believers, we know our thankfulness and praise should first be directed at God, thanking him for who he is and the promises he made to us and fulfills every day. We should be thankful for the gift of salvation and eternal life he made possible through the sacrifice of his Son on the cross. We know we should express our gratitude for the overwhelming joy, peace, and liberty this brings us. We should be thankful for the presence of the "helper" in our lives, the Holy Spirit.

We experience many good and wonderful blessings in our lives. But how often are we up to the almost "super human" challenge of expressing thankfulness and praise when things don't go our way? The challenge is remaining thankful when small things go wrong or when tragedy enters our lives.

To help us maintain a spirit of thankfulness and obedience to God's holy will, we need to ask ourselves what we gain from our experiences, whether they are good or bad in our eyes. What did we learn about ourselves, our world, our God? Did the experiences make us stronger mentally, emotionally, or spiritually?

We also need to explore how our experiences make us more compassionate, more willing to get outside ourselves and serve others. As the Apostle Paul writes in 2 Corinthians, "the Father of compassion and the God of all comfort, who comforts us in all our troubles, so that we can comfort those in any trouble with the comfort we ourselves receive from God."

So often we get caught up in ourselves and what is going wrong in our lives, that we neglect to see the difficulties others go through. There is nothing like opening our heart in service to bring on a spirit of gratitude. It's a "win-win" for everyone.

In God's Words

Give thanks to the God of heaven. His love endures forever. (Psalm 136:26)

Let the peace of Christ rule in your hearts, since as members of one body you were called to peace. And be thankful. (Colossians 3:15)

Give, and it will be given to you. A good measure, pressed down, shaken together and running over, will be poured into your lap. For with the measure you use, it will be measured to you. (Luke 6:38)

Also read: Psalm 107:1, Philippians 4:6, Colossians 4:2

In the Words of Others

"Sometimes we need to remind ourselves that thankfulness is a virtue." William Bennett

"The best way to develop the best that is in a person is by appreciation and encouragement." Charles Schwab

"The soul that gives thanks can find comfort in everything; the soul that complains can find comfort in nothing." Hannah Whitall Smith

In Your Words

Do you recall good things at night that happened that day? Do you thank the Lord for the not-so-good things?

Do you thank people on a regular basis throughout your day? Did you notice how they reacted to what you said?

Do you take time to thank the Lord for who he is and the promises he fulfills every day? Use the Psalms for inspiration.

In Your Journal

Say It. Pray It. Share It.

My God, give me a spirit of thankfulness. Help me to thank you for whatever happens in my life, for your thoughts and ways are as far above mine as heaven is above earth.

Termite Thoughts: The Silent Destroyers

In My Words

Those who work in the pest exterminating business call termites the "silent destroyers." These insects inflict an estimated $1.5 million in damage each year in the Southwest of the U.S. They can infect wood, leaf litter, soil, and animal dung. Like ants, there are workers, soldiers, kings, and of course, a queen. There are over 3,106 species of these crafty critters, and they can remain undetected until timbers rot away and collapse occurs. Then it's too late.

In a similar way, negative thoughts can burrow into our thinking and infect our emotions undetected until it's too late. We begin to feel stressed, worry more, become unproductive, experience poorer health, and lose our overall sense of well-being. These unwelcome guests become part of the fabric of who we are, affecting the way we think and act, as well as how others begin to see us.

Negative thinking patterns form like termite colonies.

You say you are a positive person, someone who always thinks the glass is half full. Think again. Experts suggest that over 80% of the thousands and thousands of our thoughts each day are negative. That is understandable since experience tells us one negative thought leads to another until the cycle is broken.

Dr. Daniel G. Amen M.D., a well-known brain disorder specialist, author of *Change Your Brain Change Your Life* and creator of ANT Therapy, identified nine types of negative thoughts, or automatic negative thoughts, including all-or-nothing thinking, over generalizing, focusing on the negative, thinking with your feelings, guilty thoughts, labeling, fortune-telling, mind-reading, and blaming.[5]

Dr. Amen notes positive thoughts release chemicals in your brain that help you feel calm and happy. He suggests the reverse is true, that negative thoughts release chemicals that make you feel stressed and unhappy. Imagine what happens when these thoughts burrow into your thinking and create patterns of negative thinking as termites create colonies. The results can include feeling down and stressed, or even a collapse into depression.

The next time you experience any of the types of negative thinking mentioned by Dr. Amen, or you discover you have your own versions of the "silent destroyers," uncover them, identify them, and replace them with positive alternatives and prayer.

Remember, as a Christian who has the mind of Christ, the best way to renew your mind, as the New Testament writer Paul suggests, is to turn to the Word of God and align your thoughts to his with the help of the Holy Spirit, who knows the mind of God and supernaturally gives you access to discern his will and ways to keep all in perspective, God's perspective.

In God's Words

Set your minds on things above, not on earthly things. (Colossians 3:2)

Trust in the LORD with all your heart and lean not on your own understanding; in all your ways submit to him, and he will make your paths straight. (Proverbs 3:5-6)

Finally, brothers and sisters, whatever is true, whatever is noble, whatever is right, whatever is pure, whatever is lovely, whatever is admirable—if anything is excellent or praiseworthy—think about such things. (Philippians 4:8)

Also read: Psalm 119:11, Proverbs 23:7, 2 Timothy 1:7

In the Words of Others

"Negativity is cannibalistic. The more you feed it, the bigger and stronger it grows." Bobby Darnell

"Stand above negativity! Dare to conquer toxic thoughts." Ernest Agyemang Yeboah

In Your Words

Recall a negative thought pattern you have. Describe the self-talk and emotions you have.

What could be a different way of thinking in those instances, a more positive pattern of thoughts and emotions?

Find a passage in the Bible that applies to experiencing negative thoughts and situations. Explore how it can help you.

In Your Journal

Say It. Pray It. Share It.

Holy Spirit, when negative thoughts emerge as I confront a challenge or an opportunity, renew my thinking so I am encouraged, dwelling on things that are worthy of praise.

Avoiding Poison Ivy People

In My Words

Over 350,000 people contract poison ivy in the U.S. every year. The nasty weed causes an itchy, irritating and sometimes painful rash. Scratching it, as I would always do as a young boy, results in it spreading across the body, as I regretfully experienced many times, also as a young boy.

My guess is far more than 350,00 people suffer from exposure each year to poison ivy people, those who cause personal irritation and pain in one way or another.

Poison ivy people with negative emotions are contagious. Being around them can drain your energy, irritate you, distract you, and waste your time. They will dump on you, causing you to worry and be anxious. The next thing you know, you are dumping on those close to you, affecting your relationships. Finding ways to avoid them or minimize your exposure will help you maintain a positive and productive life.

When you venture into the woods, you watch your step and take precautions to avoid poison ivy. You can take steps to avoid getting infected by poison ivy people. And it's just as important to know who they are as what poison ivy looks like.

To avoid infection, associate with positive people.

There are five types of poison ivy people. There are the "naysayers" who never provide encouragement because they are too busy offering discouragement. "Critics" go further as they always find fault and are not afraid to express their opinion. The "whiners" are constantly in a woe-is-me mode and thrive on pity. The "gossip" carries tales like a pro running back. The "blanket" is the person who always invades your personal space and clings to you, making you feel trapped.

To avoid infection, make a conscious effort to surround yourself with positive and productive people, and remain positive and productive yourself. Weed out negative people. If you do come in contact with a poison ivy person, whether in person or on social media, don't feel obligated to engage him or her in a lengthy conversation, argument, or stream of posts. Don't feel guilty or feel you need to offer an explanation for ending or down-sizing the relationship.

It's important to be courteous and act with Christian charity when dismissing a poison ivy person. Seek the Lord's guidance on how to proceed. It's for the Lord to judge, and the person may have their own issues that need addressed. There may be times when you can minister to the person and be a positive influence as the Lord leads you.

In God's Words

The discerning heart seeks knowledge, but the mouth of a fool feeds on folly. (Proverbs 15:14)

Do not make friends with a hot-tempered person, do not associate with one easily angered, (Proverbs 22:24)

Warn a divisive person once, and then warn them a second time. After that, have nothing to do with them. (Titus 3:10)

Also read: Proverbs 6:12-19, 1 Peter 5:8, Romans 12:2

In the Words of Others

"It's amazing how quickly things turn around when you remove toxic people from your life." Robert Tew

"You cannot expect to live a positive life if you hang with negative people." Joel Osteen

In Your Words

Think of people you know who fit the description of a poison ivy person. Describe the effects they've had on your life.

If the persons you thought of affected your life in a negative way, what could you do to end the relationship in a courteous, Christian way, or minister to them?

Have there been times when you displayed the traits of a poison ivy person and negatively affected others? Which type fits the way you acted? Why and how did you act that way?

In Your Journal

Say It. Pray It. Share It.

Lord Jesus, help me discern when to avoid a person who will negatively influence me and my relationship with you. Give me wisdom to know how to end the negative relationship or minister to the person.

Mental Magic: Overcoming Mistakes

In My Words

In sports, your ability to overcome making a mistake is crucial to success. A golfer who keeps steaming over a double bogie he made increases his chances of scoring a bogie on the next hole. A tennis player who dwells on hitting an easy return ball into the net will likely have trouble returning the next serve. In sports, having a short memory is key to maintaining focus, keeping confident, and winning.

No matter who you are or whatever your calling in life might be, you will make mistakes. The ability to perform "mental magic," and make a mistake with all its attached negative emotions disappear, is crucial to you having a positive, productive, fruitful life, and Christian walk.

Focus on all the positive things you've done.

Most of the time, we go about our lives in a confident and care-free way, not thinking much about what we normally do. When we make a mistake, it's understandable we are tempted to dwell on it, as when we have a toothache and our tongue just won't leave that tooth alone. It's natural, depending on the severity of the mistake, for our confidence and ability to be slow getting back to normal.

Whether you do something embarrassing in your personal life or make a poor decision at work, it's important for you to face it, make the required adjustments, and then move on. If sin is involved, confess it, repent of it, and ask God's forgiveness. Accept the fact that you are not perfect, a sinner, and move on.

Part of moving on is learning from our mistakes. For that reason, it is good to take time to accept responsibility for the mistake or sin, explore why it happened, and make needed

113

corrections. Learning from a mistake is different from ruminating on it and letting it dominate your thinking, negatively affecting your emotions.

When you have quiet time, prayerfully and deliberately take what you may have learned from the mistake you made, or the sin you committed, and be proactive in making sure it doesn't happen again, avoiding the circumstances that lead to it in the first place.

Once you've waved your magic mental wand and made the mistake disappear, or at least relegated it to back stage, focus on all the positive things you've recently done and watch your confidence reappear. You'll experience the freedom of mentally putting the mistake or sin behind you, and spiritually accepting the Lord's forgiveness as you move on.

In God's Words

Brothers and sisters, I do not consider myself yet to have taken hold of it. But one thing I do: Forgetting what is behind and straining toward what is ahead, (Philippians 3:13)

Though he may stumble, he will not fall, for the Lord upholds him with his hand. (Psalm 37:24)

Whoever conceals their sins does not prosper, but the one who confesses and renounces them finds mercy. (Proverbs 28:13)

Cast all your anxiety on him because he cares for you. (1 Peter 5:7)

Also read: Micah 7:8, Romans 3:23, 2 Timothy 3:16

In the Words of Others

"Isn't it nice to think that tomorrow is a new day with no mistakes in it yet?" L.M. Montgomery

"Freedom is not worth having if it does not include the freedom to make mistakes." Mahatma Gandhi

"Forgive yourself for your faults and your mistakes and move on." Les Brown

In Your Words

Can you recall a time when you kept reliving a mistake you made or a sin you committed? How did it affect your life and confidence moving on?

If you were able to move on with restored confidence in your ability to not make the same mistake or commit the sin again, how did you do it?

When you committed an act you considered to be a significant sin, were you able to confess it, repent of it, ask God's forgiveness, and move on from there? If not, why?

In Your Journal

Say It. Pray It. Share It.

Lord Jesus, I understand to make a mistake and to sin is human. But help me hold myself accountable for my actions, learn from my mistakes, and confidently carry on.

What to Do When Life Double Dares You

In My Words

Has life double dared you mentally and physically at the same time? Perhaps you were facing the prospect of opening your own business, accepting a significant but challenging promotion, or being called by God to enter some form of ministry or service. Have you faced naysayers who doubted you, and physical challenges that tested your physical abilities at the same time?

Each one of these examples includes a mental and physical dimension, a double dare, like in the 1986 *Double Dare* game show recently revived on Nickelodeon, on which kids answer challenging trivia questions and perform physical challenges.

You have the skills and knowledge to start a business, accept that promotion, or enter an area of ministry or service, but there is your old double-edged nemesis, the combination of naysayers and your fear of being able to pull it off.

David had a double-dare experience facing Goliath.

David had a double dare experience when he had to fight Goliath. The Israelites were frozen in their tracks by fear and eventually fled. But David, after being criticized and ridiculed by his brothers, told Saul he would challenge Goliath. Saul spoke a mental dare to David telling him he was only a boy and unable to confront the Philistines. David overcame this challenge by telling Saul how he fought a lion and a bear while caring for sheep.

The physical challenge for David came when he faced the nearly 10-foot-tall Goliath. The Philistine giant looked down on David and questioned why the Israelites would send a boy like David. He even cursed David and his gods. But David accepted this second dare. He announced to the Philistines that he would defeat the giant to show there was a God in Israel and the battle was God's battle, and Lord of Hosts would deliver them into the hands of the Israelites. That's exactly what happened.

The message behind the David and Goliath story is a simple one, but a hard one to fully embrace and make it an integral part of our lives. There will always be someone who will question your mental and physical capabilities to accomplish something. Ironically, that someone will often be your inner self, the part of you who is aware of past failures and worried about failing again.

The challenge we all have as Christians is to make it part of our mental, emotional, and spiritual fabric to put aside the naysayers, including our fearful inner selves, and announce to ourselves and the world by faith-powered actions that the same God in Israel, the same Lord of Hosts that David proclaimed, will be at our side as the Holy Spirit guides and strengthens us.

In God's Words

David said to the Philistine, "You come against me with sword and spear and javelin, but I come against you in the name of the LORD Almighty, the God of the armies of Israel, whom you have defied." (1 Samuel 17:45)

Have I not commanded you? Be strong and courageous. Do not be afraid; do not be discouraged, for the LORD your God will be with you wherever you go. (Joshua 1:9)

The LORD is my light and my salvation—whom shall I fear? The LORD is the stronghold of my life—of whom shall I be afraid? (Psalm 27:1)

Also Read: Isaiah 43:1, John 14:27, Philippians 4:6-7

In the Words of Others

"Prayer lets God do what he does best. Take a pebble & kill a Goliath. Take the common, make it spectacular! Pray & see what He can do." Max Lucado

"I learned that courage was not the absence of fear, but the triumph over it. The brave man is not he who does not feel afraid, but he who conquers that fear." Nelson Mandela

"The greater the obstacle, the more the glory in overcoming it." Moliere

"Fear has two meanings: 'forget everything and run' or 'face everything and rise.' The choice is yours." Zig Ziglar

In Your Words

Recall a challenge you faced in your personal or professional life that required both mental and physical strength and courage. How did you face the challenge?

Do you feel you always have to please others, especially the naysayers? Does this negatively or positively affect you? Why?

Describe how you have made God and the leading of the Holy Spirit part of how you face challenges? If not, why not?

Have you explored the scriptures on how to defeat your giants as David did by turning the battle over to God? Begin now.

In Your Journal

Say it. Pray it. Share it.

Father God, give me wisdom to discern your holy and true will when those around me are advising me on my path ahead. Holy Spirit, give me the strength and courage to follow the Father's direction.

Thinking Outside *Your* Box

In My Words

When I was a child, I pretended I was a spaceman. I'm sure my backyard adventures were inspired by watching the exploits of Flash Gordon on the TV series in the 1950s.

I would collect a couple cardboard boxes and build a space ship. I would crawl inside the biggest box and slouch down to begin my space travels as I closed the lid over my head. While inside the box, I would imagine outside the box, traveling to unknown planets among the stars. I was just being a kid, thinking and imagining without boundaries.

Much has been written about thinking outside the box from a business management and success standpoint. This phrase is used to indicate creatively thinking about a problem from a different perspective and doing so without boundaries. Brainstorming is a tool often used to gather ideas outside the box.

In reality, thinking outside the box is thinking outside *your* personal box, outside *your* mindset at the time. The term "mindset" indicates our minds have set patterns, ways of thinking formed over the years. Mindsets are inherently limiting.

Be a personal brain stormer open to new ideas.

When sitting in a brainstorming session in a business environment, we can participate easily in the free flow of ideas from associates. But thinking and brainstorming outside *your* personal box is more challenging. Ironically, developing a mindset of thinking outside *your* box is needed.

To think outside *your* box, you need to adopt a mindset of unlimited possibilities embracing an openness to whole new experiences. Be a mental and emotional brain stormer open to new ideas, and unwilling to automatically discard ideas.

Enhance this mindset by getting comfortable with the unexpected, doing new things, and experiencing new people and places. Eliminate the internal or external naysayers that always advise caution.

This way of thinking has implications for the way you approach goalsetting. Setting goals and objectives is inherently creating a box within which certain actions take place. The key phrase to remember is "mindful flexibility," the ability to always be alert in the present to consider new and different ways to accomplish the same goals as things change.

There are spiritual implications to this way of thinking. Even a cursory reading of the New Testament and parts of the Old Testament that foretold parts of Jesus' life, leaves no doubt Jesus not only acted outside the box, he created a whole new box, a gift box of eternal proportions that revolutionized the world.

Like the cardboard box I slouched in as a child that allowed me to imagine boundless possibilities, the box each of us can claim, and act upon as believers, is only bound by God's boundless riches.

In God's Words

I will do what you have asked. I will give you a wise and discerning heart, so that there will never have been anyone like you, nor will there ever be. (1 Kings 3:12)

"For my thoughts are not your thoughts, neither are your ways my ways," declares the LORD. "As the heavens are higher than the earth, so are my ways higher than your ways and my thoughts than your thoughts." (Isaiah 55:8-9)

So, from now on we regard no one from a worldly point of view. Though we once regarded Christ in this way, we do so no longer. Therefore, if anyone is in Christ, the new creation has come: The old has gone, the new is here! (2 Corinthians 5:16-17)

Also read: Luke 1:37, Romans 2:1, 1 Corinthians 3:18

In the Words of Others

"Big ideas come from forward thinking people who challenge the norm, think outside the box, and invent the world they see inside rather than submitting to the limitations of current dilemmas." J. D. Jakes

"It's easier to think outside the box if you don't draw one around yourself." Jason Kravits

"Without leaps of imagination, or dreaming, we lose the excitement of possibilities. Dreaming, after all, is a form of planning." Gloria Steinem

In Your Words

Recall when you thought outside *your* box. What process did you follow? How did you become a personal brain stormer?

Think of times when you tried to be creative and your internal naysayer started naysaying. Recall your self-talk.

Have there been times when you prayed for a solution and things unexpectedly worked out? Were you also brainstorming yourself at the time? How did you feel about that?

In Your Journal

Say It. Pray It. Share It.

Holy Spirit, I pray you inspire me when I am confronted with problems for which I have no answer. You alone connect me with the unfathomable mind of God, where endless creativity abounds.

Getting Comfy Outside Your Comfort Zone

In My Words

On a recent vacation in Cancun, Mexico, I had to literally jump outside my comfort zone as I faced a 40-foot drop from a cliff into the clear surface waters of a cenote, a network of underwater caves and caverns. On my way up to the cliff, I felt very comfortable with the jump, having dove off high dive boards many times. But this was to be different.

After peering over the edge and seeing all my companions down below urging me on, I froze. After three tries at talking myself into jumping off the cliff, I made the leap and embarrassed myself with my fellow travelers below as I raised one leg, turning a #10 descent into a #2 back flop. Ouch! Double ouch!!

After I climbed up the rugged stone path out of the cenote pool, one of my companions tried to mitigate my embarrassment and pain by saying, "At least you did it." I thought, "Yes, I did it."

God is waiting for us at the edge of our comfort zone.

Despite the redness and stinging on my back, I felt great. But while the experience was an example of someone stepping (jumping) outside their comfort zone, it certainly wasn't comfy.

As my less than perfect cenote experience demonstrated, going outside your comfort zone can have its ups and downs (literally for me).

Our comfort zone is a psychological state in which we feel at ease with what is going on around us and what we are doing. We feel little stress and are able to productively accomplish what needs to be done. Life feels good.

124

By going outside your comfort zone, two things happen. On the up side, you are living beyond what you've thought possible for you. You are thinking beyond your natural abilities. As you live this way, you expand your comfort zone, experiencing new things, new adventures, and personal growth.

There is stress involved, but if kept in check, it is a small price to pay for the growth you can experience. However, on the down side, when you go too far outside your comfort zone, pushing too hard beyond what you can realistically accomplish, anxiety and stress mount to a point where your enjoyment and productivity suffer, and your personal growth can be stunted.

When you make a habit of thoughtfully stepping outside your comfort zone by trying different things and pursuing new experiences, you can become more willing to push your personal boundaries, more productive, more comfortable with the unexpected, and more creative.

Where is God in all this?

He is waiting at the edge of your comfort zone, telling you that you should not look at life challenges and opportunities from the standpoint of what YOU can do or should do. He wants you to measure your ability to do things against what he can do, and what you can do with his help. As you prayerfully trust him and believe in his Word, you will also trust yourself more, and be more comfy living outside your comfort zone.

In God's Words

Have I not commanded you? Be strong and courageous. Do not be afraid; do not be discouraged, for the LORD your God will be with you wherever you go. (Joshua 1:9)

You did not choose me, but I chose you and appointed you so that you might go and bear fruit—fruit that will last—and so that whatever you ask in my name the Father will give you. (John 15:16)

Do not merely listen to the word, and so deceive yourselves. Do what it says. (James 1:22)

Also read: Proverbs 28:1, Jeremiah 29:11-14, Romans 12:1-2

In the Words of Others

"You never change your life until you step out of your comfort zone. Change begins at the end of your comfort zone." Roy T. Bennett

"Life is a concept, like the 'universe,' that expands as soon as we reach what we think is its edge." Kamand Kajoouri

"You must always overcome your comfort zone." Sunday Adelaja

In Your Words

Recall times you stepped outside your comfort zone. In what way did they expand your comfort zone and result in your growth?

Was there a time when you couldn't bring yourself to step outside your comfort zone? What prevented you from doing so?

Have you ever explored outside your comfort zone too far and too quickly? Describe what happened.

How was the Lord involved in your venturing outside your comfort zone? Did you turn to him in prayer for guidance?

In Your Journal

Say It. Pray It. Share It.

Holy Spirit, give me the wisdom to know when to step outside my comfort zone as I serve the Father and others around me. Give me the courage to do so despite any challenges I might face.

Overworking Your Good Intentions

In My Words

Each of us is blessed with God-given talents and resources with which we can be a blessing and of service to others. But as Aesop once asked, "Is it possible to have too much of a good thing?" Can we serve too much? Can we overwork our good intentions?

Behind every good intention is a desire to help. Behind every desire to help are God-given strengths, acquired skills, and life experiences that make you who you are, and give you the ability and confidence to make good on your intentions. However, not all efforts spawned by good intentions are beneficial.

Hell is not necessarily paved with good intentions, as the saying goes, but overworking your good intentions can pave a slippery slope with the oil of negative consequences when you get trapped into doing too much at the expense of your physical, social, emotional, mental, and spiritual well-being.

Serving too much, the wrong way, at the wrong time.

There are the "go-getters" who tackle a project with 120% effort, devoting all their time and energy to accomplishing what needs to get done. They invest themselves in making things happen, and accomplishing goals and objectives at all costs. Unfortunately, they often fail to count the costs to their physical and mental well-being, their families, and their spiritual welfare. I am the last person to minimize the importance of volunteerism. However, I've seen cases of volunteer "burnout" caused by persons getting deeply involved in one service project after another.

You would think the Lord would want you to spend as much time as possible serving in church. But when participating in church activities overshadows the reason for serving and the idea of accomplishing things becomes the idol, you spend less time with the person for whom you are serving, the Lord our God.

There are many things as Christians and right-thinking persons we should be doing, but that doesn't mean we should do them all or do them at the expense of our physical and mental well-being, our families, and our relationship with God. There is such a thing as serving too much, serving in the wrong way, serving at the wrong time, and serving for the wrong reason.

As Martha learned from Jesus in Luke 10:38-42, being caught up in activity and anxious about servicing distracts us from attending to the "good portion" in our lives. It is important we do three things before acting on our good intentions to serve. We need to prepare ourselves for service of any kind, plan how our service fits into our lives, and most importantly, pray about it before making a commitment.

In God's Words

He has shown you, O mortal, what is good. And what does the LORD require of you? To act justly and to love mercy and to walk humbly with your God. (Micah 6:8)

A generous person will prosper; whoever refreshes others will be refreshed. (Proverbs 11:25)

For by the grace given me I say to every one of you: Do not think of yourself more highly than you ought, but rather think of yourself with sober judgment, in accordance with the faith God has distributed to each of you. (Romans 12:3)

Also read: Matthew 6:1-4, Luke 10:38-42, Romans 7:13-25

In the Words of Others

"Good intentions but bad results; bad results but lessons learned. There is a dark corner on every task beautiful and a beautiful corner on every task dark." Criss Jami

"Good intentions might sound nice, but it's positive actions that matter." Tim Fargo

In Your Words

Was there a time when you became so involved in a project that you taxed your physical well-being and family relationships? Describe what you could have done differently.

Did you ever lose sight of why you volunteered in the first place? If it was a church project, how was God served?

Have you ever suffered from volunteer "burnout?" Why did it happen and what could you have done differently?

In Your Journal

Say It. Pray It. Share It.

Father God, thank you for the resources you have given me. Help me use them wisely as I serve you by serving others.

Facing Crisis: A Life-Changing Experience

In My Words

Sir Isaac Newton postulated in his Third Law of Motion, that in every interaction there is a pair of forces acting on the two interacting objects. He said the forces on the two objects will be the same. This idea is also central to the law of Karma, which states that when we speak, act and even think, we begin a force that reacts accordingly and returns to us in some way, kind of a natural boomerang or "tit for tat."

In life, our experiences affect the way we react. And the way we react affects the way we experience. This is a fundamental circular life process that begins in the womb. How does this apply to the way we experience life-changing situations, crises that cause us to turn from our everyday concerns and ask deep questions about who we are, why we are here, and the meaning of life?

God is the great equalizing force in times of crisis.

It could be the death of a loved one, a near-death experience, loss of a long-time job, word of a terminal illness, a destructive hurricane, or a terrorist attack. These traumatic experiences bring us before the intellectual, emotional, and spiritual mirror of our lives and invite us to stare into it, painfully deep into it. In some cases, we get angry with God and question our faith, leading us further down a hole in guilt.

How we effectively react to trauma and recover from its effects over time depends on many factors, including how we have experienced and reacted to other life-changing experiences, and the support system we have in place, especially our relationship with God. He is the great equalizing force that helps us navigate through crisis.

We all react differently to these types of experiences that can deeply affect us for weeks, months, or even years. If we ignore the significance of the experiences all together, perhaps brushing them off as bumps in the road of life, or even denying they happened, this could be an unconscious defensive reaction.

Professionals in the field of personal, emergency, and group crisis management suggest the first step in the process of recovering from a traumatic experience, and eventually positively living a "new normal," is to admit it happened and your reaction to it is "normal." This is called normalizing the experience.

Crisis volunteers and professionals who serve on the ground or spend time in counseling sessions, will also suggest how even non-believers, when in the throes of a crisis, will often turn to God, even if only in supplication or anger.

As believers, we understand God's promises in his Word unequivocally state he will equalize the effects of any force that comes against us. With the Lord in our hearts and the Holy Spirit at your side, you can weather and even benefit from life's storms, as an opportunity to personally grow, and grow closer to God.

In God's Words

God is our refuge and strength, an ever-present help in trouble. (Psalm 46:1)

Trust in the LORD with all your heart and lean not on your own understanding; in all your ways submit to him, and he will make your paths straight.
(Proverbs 3:5-6)

Consider it pure joy, my brothers and sisters, whenever you face trials of many kinds, because you know that the testing of your faith produces perseverance. Let perseverance finish its work so that you may be mature and complete, not lacking anything. (James 1:2-4)

Also read: Psalm 23:1-6, John 14:1, Philippians 4:6-7

In the Words of Others

"You gain strength, courage, and confidence by every experience in which you really stop to look fear in the face. You are able to say to yourself, 'I lived through the horror. I can take the next thing that comes along.'" Eleanor Roosevelt

"When written in Chinese, the word crisis is composed of two characters...one represents danger, and the other represents opportunity." John F. Kennedy

In Your Words

Have you had a significant crisis, a life-changing experience? What are the details? What was your immediate reaction?

Did the experience change your life? How do you think this experience affected the way you would react to other life-changing experiences?

What role did God play in how you reacted? Even if you may have been angry with God, how did he help you going forward, perhaps finding meaning in what you experienced?

In Your Journal

Say It. Pray It. Share It.

Holy Spirit, I pray those who experience crisis will turn to you. It is through you they can walk through troubled waters and not drown, and walk through fire and not be set ablaze.

Finding Your Life Purpose on Purpose

In My Words

Motivation and business gurus suggest we should have an "elevator speech," a concise, brief message about ourselves that communicates who we are and what we do to benefit a company or organization. It's like a commercial we create for ourselves, one we can deliver in the time it takes to ride from the top to the bottom of a building in an elevator, about 30 seconds.

The creation of an elevator speech is not an easy thing to do. It begins with a thoughtful process in which we answer a combination of the who, what, why, when, where, and how questions. It ends with a difficult and purposeful editing process, difficult because most of us like to talk about ourselves.

The creation of a "life purpose speech" is a deliberate process of answering fundamental questions about who we are, and what we should do to fulfill our God-given purpose in life. While many people go about their lives haphazardly living from day to day without having a clue about what God wants them to accomplish, you have an opportunity to find your life purpose **on purpose**.

A mosaic that tells you who God wants you to be.

You are the way you are for a reason. You've experienced what you have for a reason. Who you are, what you have experienced, and what drives you to act, all play a role in determining how you fulfill God's purpose for you. Once you prayerfully complete your life purpose speech, you can be confident God is directing you because he doesn't make mistakes.

The answers you discover form a mosaic that tells you who God wants you to be and his purpose for you. Once you define your God-given purpose and determine whether or not your life aligns with it, you can make adjustments going forward to align your life with your purpose, your destiny. You'll have made a deliberate effort to obey God as you walk a path predestined for you.

You will be able to answer these core questions: How can I live out God's purpose for me in all areas of my life? How will I make sure I keep on track? And, who will be there to support me? If you walk in prayerful obedience to God, he will provide answers to these questions and the resources you need to fulfill your life destiny.

In God's Words

The LORD Almighty has sworn, "Surely, as I have planned, so it will be, and as I have purposed, so it will happen." (Isaiah 14:24)

And we know that in all things God works for the good of those who love him, who have been called according to his purpose. (Romans 8:28)

But seek first his kingdom and his righteousness, and all these things will be given to you as well. (Matthew 6:33)

Also read: Psalm 119:105, Jeremiah 29:11, 1 Corinthians 7:17

In the Words of Others

"To serve is beautiful, but only if it is done with joy and a whole heart and a free mind." Pearl S. Buck

"The purpose of life is to contribute in some way to making things better." Robert F. Kennedy

"If you know that God loves you, you should never question a directive from him." Henry Blackaby

In Your Words

What is your current position, where you are today in how you live your life? Your Christian walk?

What are your abilities and skills that help you achieve?

What experiences and education have been part of your successes?

What are you really passionate about? What values and principles guide you?

Who have you been able to serve over the years? About what aspects of your service have you been most passionate?

What is your purpose in life? Write a brief "life purpose speech."

In Your Journal

Say It. Pray It. Share It.

Father God, you placed me on this earth for a reason. Help me open my mind and heart to discover the reason, and fulfill my God-given purpose.

Connecting Your Life's Dots

In My Words

One of my favorite puzzle activities as a child was connecting the dots. The activity is also called dot to dot and join the dots. I always anticipated seeing the big picture once all the numbers were connected. Connecting the dots has also become a favorite activity of the media, politicians, and law enforcement officials when they refer to an ongoing story or investigation. It seems like they're always trying to connect the dots to figure out what's going on in their world.

We all encounter times in our lives when we struggle to connect the dots, scratching our heads as we try to make sense of things that just don't make sense in our personal and professional lives. Ironically, this activity can be a useful exercise to help us connect parts of our past as we try to hone in on the right path going forward.

Life is never a meaningless collection of happenings.

Someone created the connect-the-dots puzzles I used to enjoy. That person had a picture in mind as he or she positioned the dots and corresponding numbers on the page. The picture could have been a flower, an animal, or a country scene. In the same way, God visualizes our lives before we are born. To us, our lives may seem to be a meaningless collection of happenings, and we will probably never see the whole picture until we are in heaven. To the Lord, our God, it all makes perfect sense since he is a perfect God, and he created our life puzzle.

Thoughtfully and prayerfully begin connecting your life's dots to know more about who you really are, what you should be doing today and going forward in your life, and your spiritual journey. These dots could include courses you took, useful skills you acquired, jobs you accepted, friends you made, and any of the other major and not-so-major decisions you made in your life.

When you face a major decision in your life or consider how to fulfill your life purpose, take out a plain sheet of paper and randomly write keywords representing your past life dots. Make no judgement regarding their value. When finished, connect the keywords that relate to each other and brainstorm the keywords, allowing a mental picture to emerge and how it applies to the decision you face. Take what you've discovered to the Lord in prayer. Ask for the guidance of the Holy Spirit.

In God's Words

"For I know the plans I have for you," declares the LORD, "plans to prosper you and not to harm you, plans to give you hope and a future." (Jeremiah 29:11)

And we know that in all things God works for the good of those who love him, who have been called according to his purpose. (Romans 8:28)

Also read: Ephesians 2:10, Job 42:2, Proverbs 19:21

In the Words of Others

"Because believing that all the dots will connect down the road will give you the confidence to follow your heart, even when it leads you off the well-worn path." Steve Jobs

"If we don't manage to connect the dots anymore and the power of our imagination is creaking at the seams,

in a world of withering expectations, we have to rewrite the script of our life." Erik Pevernagie

In Your Words

If you used the keyword exercise mentioned above, how did you feel about it? What did you discover about yourself and what you should be doing in life? What themes emerged?

What keywords did you use to describe successes in the various areas of your life? What God-given strengths and abilities helped you?

What keywords would you use to describe the skills you acquired along the way to help you?

Were there any keywords or phrases that stirred up memories about activities or causes that energized you?

If asked about the role God played in your successes and ability to discover and fulfill your life purpose, what would you say?

In Your Journal

Say It. Pray It. Share It.

Father God, you alone know everything about my past, present, and future. I pray you help me discern how I can learn from my past and apply its lessons as I serve you and others.

Being a Bug in the Rug of Life

In My Words

The "bug in a rug" expression is believed to date back to 1769 and comes from the image of a moth larva resting happily inside a rolled-up rug. When applied to the mundane activities of life with its unexpected twists, turns, and temptations that distract us from being who the Lord wants us to be, and doing what he wants us to do, it can feel like we are not a very comfortable "bug in a rug."

Let's look at this expression from a different angle. Consider the rug. Better yet, let's think of it as a fine tapestry, an image more appropriate for the magnificent artistry God has demonstrated in creation.

Watch for God's golden strands of involvement.

I'm sure there have been many sermons preached comparing our lives to a tapestry. One way of looking at this image is to stand back from the tapestry and see the overall fine beauty of life with all its magnificent designs and colors. This is God's perspective, and only God's as the artistic creator and sustainer of our lives, with its rich colors and hues. Another approach is to look at the back of the tapestry. From this view, as disorganized and tangled as it might appear, we can appreciate the handiwork that went into the tapestry's creation. This is seeing God as the craftsman.

The third way of looking at tapestry is from our everyday perspective, being that "bug in a rug" amidst all the strands of fiber. We need to pause and look around us. We need to watch for God's golden strands of involvement through the working of the Holy Spirit in our past, and as we go about our daily lives. It's easier to see these in retrospect when we're not navigating around the fibers of our daily lives.

When looking at them in the past, we can come closer to seeing what is going on in our life, and how God is working from his overall perspective, and appreciate his artistry in the details, bringing people and events into our lives.

Take time for solitude and some form of meditation. This will allow you opportunities to look for themes and ways God moved in your life, weaving people and events into your life. God will bring them to your mind. Pay attention to your dreams. Your dreams are a collection of past, present and perhaps even future experiences. The Bible has many examples of dreams and how God communicates through them.

Now and then, look back on your life and write a short story about certain experiences. Don't worry about grammar or spelling. Just let the creative juices flow. Make up your mind you will learn from the past, even though the lessons may be painful. Sometimes God's golden strands reflect pain and suffering. These strands can often be the most valuable.

In God's Word

But the LORD said to Samuel, "Do not consider his appearance or his height, for I have rejected him. The LORD does not look at the things people look at. People look at the outward appearance, but the LORD looks at the heart." (1 Samuel 16:7)

Jesus replied, "You do not realize now what I am doing, but later you will understand." (John 13:7)

For our light and momentary troubles are achieving for us an eternal glory that far outweighs them all. (2 Corinthians 4:17)

Also read: Psalm 19:1-4, Isaiah 14:27, 1 Samuel 12:16

In the Words of Others

"Losers live in the past. Winners learn from the past and enjoy working in the present toward the future."
Denis Waitley

"If you spend your life over analyzing every encounter you will always see the tree, but never the forest."
Shannon L. Alder

In Your Words

Do you have a diary or journal? If you do, how often do you review it? Describe any themes you found and ways God moved in your life, bringing people and events in and out of your life.

Have you found times for solitude and some form of meditation? Again, describe ways these times have helped you discover ways God moved in your life.

Have you paid attention to your dreams? How have they been a collection of your experiences? Write a short narrative describing one or two such dreams.

In Your Journal

Say It. Pray It. Share It.

Lord God, help me discern how you are working in my life. Give me the strength to obediently be an actor in the story you want to tell through the life you designed for me.

Getting Off on the Right Floor

In My Words

I've found it amazing how many times I've walked through an open elevator door only to realize I was getting off on the wrong floor. And I know I'm not alone. Just this morning, I entered an elevator and greeted an elderly couple. A few minutes later, they walked out when the elevator door opened, and had to walk back in embarrassed and apologetic because it was the wrong floor.

The thought occurred to me after assuring the couple they caused no inconvenience, that the Lord has wired each one of us to walk through open doors, especially opportunity doors through which he wants us to walk. It also occurred to me that just like me and the elderly couple, we sometimes go through the wrong door at the right time or the right door at the wrong time.

Be patient, willing to wait for the right opportunity.

When we do go through the wrong opportunity doors, it's often because we are doing so for the wrong reasons, or following people who are doing something completely different for different reasons. We are not paying attention to what we should be doing or where we should be going.

You need to know where you're going and why. When you get on an elevator and push a button, you hopefully know which floor you are getting off and are willing to wait until you reach the correct floor. It's the same way with pursuing God-given opportunities. You have to be patient, willing to wait for the right opportunity door at the right time, God's time.

When you're looking for opportunities in life, you need to know the kind of opportunities for which you are looking. Knowing who you are and what you want to accomplish in life, especially in your Christian walk, will help you seize the right opportunities at the right time. Patience is key when waiting on the Lord to open the right doors for you. Prayer and being in God's Word are essential in determining which opportunities to pursue.

Sometimes you have to be ready to get off the elevator on a different floor than you anticipated. A number of times elevator doors opened and I saw an old friend, an unexpected joy. In the same way, we have to be open to opportunities that appear unexpectedly. At other times, the Lord surprises us, bringing people and events into our lives unexpectedly that will affect the path we take. Again, prayerful discernment is key to making the right move at the right time, according to the Lord's time.

In God's Words

He who gathers crops in summer is a prudent son, but he who sleeps during harvest is a disgraceful son. (Proverbs 10:5)

There is a time for everything, and a season for every activity under the heavens: (Ecclesiastes 3:1)

Let us not become weary in doing good, for at the proper time we will reap a harvest if we do not give up. Therefore, as we have opportunity, let us do good to all people, especially to those who belong to the family of believers. (Galatians 6:9-10)

Also read: Psalm 139, Ephesians 5:16, Matthew 25:1-46

In the Words of Others

"Life is like an elevator, up and down. Just make sure you get off at the right floor." Keith Douglas

"Some say opportunity only knocks once. That is not true. Opportunity knocks all the time, but you have to be ready for it. If the chance comes, you must have the equipment to take advantage of it." Louis L'Amour

"God's timing is always perfect. Trust his delays. He's got you." Tony Evans

In Your Words

List opportunities of which you took advantage. Describe how they turned out. Was timing a factor in your decision? Describe how.

Recall reasons why you missed opportunities. What could you have done differently? Was timing a factor? Explain how.

List opportunities you face. How do you take advantage of them? Will God be part of your discernment process?

In Your Journal

Say It. Pray It. Share It.

Holy Spirit, help me discern and take advantage of the opportunities the Lord creates for me in both the earthly and spiritual realms to serve him and others.

Making Failure Your Friend

I love chocolate. So, I was excited when we decided to visit the Hershey plant in Hershey, PA. The tour of Hershey's Chocolate World was amazing, but the Trolley Works tour around the historic town of Hershey was inspiring. The trolley conductor told the story of Milton Snavley Hershey, founder of the Hershey Company and the town bearing his name.

As a Christian life coach, I was fascinated to learn how Hershey had two business failures before he was successful at starting his chocolate business, and how success became a blessing for the small Pennsylvania community.

Hershey was an entrepreneur who believed in taking care of his company's workers and building a community that would serve them. Out of this belief came his efforts to start the Milton Hershey School Trust Fund and the M. S. Hershey Foundation, a private charitable foundation that to this day provides educational and cultural opportunities for thousands of people, including at-risk children.

It's a matter of how we react to failure that counts.

The well-known confectioner exemplifies someone who made failure his friend as he learned from his failures, didn't give up, and was blessed to be a blessing to others. He was especially blessed when he and his wife, Kitty, cancelled at the last minute their plans to sail on the ill-fated maiden voyage of the RMS Titanic.

We often look at failure as an enemy, something to avoid at all costs. I believe this is not just a natural inclination, but a God-given drive to be the very best we can be. Failure will happen to each of us at some point and in some way in our lives. The question is not if failure will happen, it is a matter of how we react to it. Will we see it as an enemy or as a friend?

Failure often tells us what we need to know about ourselves, and like a good friend, it doesn't "sugar coat" its message. It challenges us. If we pay attention to what it's telling us, it teaches us why we failed, what we should have done differently, and that failure is not the end of the world and life goes on.

Whether we fail at times in our personal or professional lives, we have to dig inside ourselves, as Hershey did, and explore where the disappointment of failure intersects with the satisfaction of discovering new opportunities and hope. We have to adopt the mindset that refuses to equate our identity with failure. We fail, but we are not failures.

The greatest example of someone who failed in the eyes of the world and his followers, and who became a blessing and source of hope to others, was Jesus Christ. How could anyone who stood at the foot of the cross believe Jesus was a success? If only they knew the rest of the story.

In God's Words

But he said to me, "My grace is sufficient for you, for my power is made perfect in weakness." Therefore, I will boast all the more gladly about my weaknesses, so that Christ's power may rest on me. (2 Corinthians 12:9)

Not only so, but we also glory in our sufferings, because we know suffering produces perseverance; perseverance, character; and character, hope. And hope does not put us to shame, because God's love has been poured out into our hearts through the Holy Spirit, who has been given to us. (Romans 5:3-5)

Also read: Joshua 1:9, 1 Peter 5:6-7, Philippians 4:13

In the Words of Others

"Success is not final, failure is not fatal: it is the courage to continue that counts." Winston Churchill

"Negative results are just what I want. They're just as valuable to me as positive results. I can never find the thing that does the job best until I find the ones that don't." Thomas Edison

"Failure is a detour, not a dead-end street." Zig Ziglar

In Your Words

Recall a time when you failed in your personal or professional life. Describe how you felt at the time. Did you see yourself as someone who failed or as a failure?

Can you cite an example of when you failed at something and it opened up new opportunities? If so, describe how.

Learn about those who failed but later succeeded and became a blessing to others. Consider King David and Elijah, and St. Peter and St. Paul in the New Testament.

In Your Journal

Say It. Pray It. Share It.

Lord Jesus, help me be the best I can be. Help see a failure as an opportunity to grow and be a blessing and help to others.

Low Beams vs. High Beams

In My Words

I'm sure you've realized by now it's much better to drive with your low beams on in the fog than to use your high beams. That idea struck me the other day as a natural teaching moment when I was driving early in the morning through a dense fog. The conditions forced me to use my low beams, slow down, and concentrate on the road in front of me.

This is how we have to approach our daily lives, being proactively and intentionally aware, and involved in the present moment---being mindful of the present. This living in the moment is what is called mindfulness. Even when we have short- and long-term goals, we accomplish them by meeting objectives one at a time, in the present moment.

Sometimes you need to slow down, focus on the now.

We often focus too much on the future with all the possible twists and turns, unexpected obstacles, and places to go and things to do. It's like entering a foggy stretch on the road. Sometimes it's important to slow down, take a deep breath, and focus on the now, the road in front of you.

When you make every moment of your day matter as much as possible, concentrating on what you should be doing at that time, it is a way to make sure you are headed in the right direction in whatever you are doing. When driving in the fog, if you patiently focus on the road you can see, you reach your destination safely.

Looking at the fog metaphor from another perspective, consider the crystallized moisture that hovers before you while you are driving as a spiritual calmness and not as a foreboding event. Consider it to be the Lord inviting you to be at peace with the present while you move forward in life, focusing on what is important and not all the distractions that leap out at us from life's berms, side roads, and ditches.

If you have distracting thoughts about all the things you have to accomplish that day, look at them as part of the scenery along the roadside and then pass them by, not giving them a second thought. When you rise in the morning, take a deep breath, turn to the Lord, and ask him to help you concentrate on what is **REALLY** important to him that day and keeping you successfully on the path of life he has chosen for you.

In God's Words

Therefore, do not worry about tomorrow, for tomorrow will worry about itself. Each day has enough trouble of its own. (Matthew 6:34)

Let your eyes look straight ahead; fix your gaze directly before you. (Proverbs 4:25)

Your word is a lamp for my feet, a light on my path. (Psalm 119:105)

Also read: Proverbs 16:3, Romans 8:5, James 1:22-25

In the Words of Others

"Yesterday is history, tomorrow is a mystery, today is a gift of God, which is why we call it the present." Bill Keane

"Be happy in the moment, that's enough. Each moment is all we need, not more." Mother Teresa

"I love a broad margin to my life. Sometimes, in a summer morning, having taken my accustomed bath, I sat in my sunny doorway from sunrise till noon, rapt in a reverie." Henry David Thoreau

In Your Words

Have there been times you became distracted instead of concentrating on the task at hand? If yes, what were the consequences?

When you lose focus on the present and begin worrying about what is going to happen in the future, how does this affect your personal or professional life?

How have you been able to be mindfully present in your personal or professional life? If not, how do you propose to change?

Cite specific instances when being in the now benefited you in your personal or professional life? In your Christian walk? How will you keep the Lord involved in the process?

In Your Journal

Say It. Pray It. Share It.

Holy Spirit, help me keep my priorities in line with the Father's will, and not be distracted by my own emotionally based worries and concerns about the future.

What If You Won 2,207,520,000?

In My Words

On January 13, 2016, three people learned they had the winning ticket in a record $1.5 billion Powerball lottery. They sure were lucky. However, I think each of us, the moment we are born, have the ability to potentially shatter that record.

Notice the title of this article is missing something---a dollar sign.

The average life span of a person is 70 years. Leaving out leap years, that equates to 2,207,520,000 seconds. Obviously, some people don't live 70 years and others live much longer. But at the moment of conception each one of us has the potential of possessing something far more valuable than money---billions of seconds in time.

God awards us a set amount of time to serve him.

If you live a long life, you can be a big winner. But just as with those who win huge lotteries, the kind of winner you are is determined by what you do with your winnings, how you manage all those precious seconds, for your benefit only or for serving others as God leads you.

When you manage your time, you are managing yourself, maximizing the gift of life God has given you. There are several key principles of time management. These include prioritizing your activities, planning your activities, and performing your activities at the times of the day when your life rhythms are at their maximum effectiveness.

God awards each of us a set amount of time. It's a gift not to be squandered as unmanaged time. It's important that we prioritize our activities and budget our time, counting the cost of performing activities. Equally important is counting the cost of not performing them.

Keeping a journal is an excellent way to see exactly how you manage your time and activities. It will help you make needed adjustments in your daily routines, establish new routines and stick to them, and identify people who are "time thieves."

While serving others is important, learn to say "no" as the Lord leads you. The Bible has much to say about how we should prayerfully seek to discern God's will. As we plan how to use our time, doing God's will should always be priority number one.

In God's Words

Be wise in the way you act toward outsiders; make the most of every opportunity. (Colossians 4:5)

Suppose one of you wants to build a tower. Won't you first sit down and estimate the cost to see if you have enough money to complete it? (Luke 14:28)

Therefore, my dear brothers and sisters, stand firm. Let nothing move you. Always give yourselves fully to the work of the Lord, because you know that your labor in the Lord is not in vain. (1 Corinthians 15:58)

Also read: Proverbs 16:9, James 4:13-17, Ephesians 5:15-17

In the Words of Others

"Your greatest resource is your time." Brian Tracy

"Time is the most valuable coin in your life. You and you alone will determine how that coin will be spent. Be careful that you do not let other people spend it for you." Carl Sandburg

"No one has more time than you have. It is the discipline and stewardship of your time that is important. The management of time is the management of self; therefore, if you manage time with God, he will begin to manage you." Jill Briscoe

In Your Words

How would you rate your current time management on a scale of 1-10? Describe why?

At what time of the day are you most productive? How will knowing this improve your productivity?

Describe how you prioritize what your activities will be for the day, for the week. Do you need to make changes?

Do you go before the Lord in prayer for guidance as you plan your time? Describe when and how you do this.

In Your Journal

Say It. Pray It. Share It.

Father God, you awarded me a limited number of seconds on earth. Help me to cherish each day as a window of opportunity to serve you and accomplish what you will for me.

Playing Pin Your Tale to Your Passions

In My Words

I remember playing pin the tail on the donkey at birthday parties as a child. After being blindfolded and spun around I had to navigate around chairs and other kids to pin the tail on a paper donkey. And I had to do this without peeking. I usually pinned everything and everybody but the paper donkey.

This party game is a fitting metaphor for meeting challenges we face when we try to discover and live our God-given calling and purpose. We often have trouble following the path God called us to follow when we allow the spinning whirlpool of life events and distractions to blind and confuse us, misdirecting us as we pin our hopes and dreams to meaningless paper life donkeys.

A tale created by the greatest author of all time.

Each one of us is living a tale created by the greatest author who ever lived, God. Our tale is the story created by all the influences and experiences affecting our lives from birth. Some of the most significant influences creating our storyline are our passions, the internal drives that energize us.

Our passions are a product of how our God-given abilities and gifts mold our experiences, and how our experiences in turn fashion the use of our abilities and gifts. The more we use our abilities and gifts in a useful and successful way, the more passionate we become about them. We experience the satisfaction of doing something well. We are energized and emotionally bond to the experience.

When you identify your core passions in life, you are one step closer to discovering your life purpose and following your storyline written by God. An excellent way of identifying your passions is to sit down and review your life, searching for the experiences that brought you deep satisfaction and energized you, not just passing pleasures.

Once you identify activities and experiences about which you are passionate, those that motivate you and energize you throughout your day despite distractions, you will have a better idea of what the Lord wants you to do with your life.

Prayerfully go before the Lord and be in his Word. Ask the Holy Spirit to help you take what you've learned from your past storyline and pin it to your future storyline, your tale yet to be told, to your passions as you discern your calling and God's purpose for you in life.

In God's Words

In their hearts, humans plan their course, but the Lord establishes their steps. (Proverbs 16:9)

The purposes of a person's heart are deep waters, but one who has insight draws them out. (Proverbs 20:5)

Whatever you do, work at it with all your heart, as working for the Lord, not for human masters,
(Colossians 3:23)

Also read: Deuteronomy 6:5, Proverbs 19:21, Philippians 4:13

In the Words of Others

"Passion is energy. Feel the power that comes from focusing on what excites you." Oprah Winfrey

157

"If you can't figure out your purpose, figure out your passion. For your passion will lead you right into your purpose." Bishop T.D. Jakes

In Your Words

About what have you been passionate? What activities or accomplishments have energized you and given you true joy, not just passing pleasure?

If you had unlimited time, money and other resources, what are the three things you would do without hesitation?

If you were told you had three months to live, what three things would you make sure you experienced or accomplished?

Reflect on what your answers tell you about how God designed you and what he wants you to accomplish in your life.

In Your Journal

Say It. Pray It. Share It.

Holy Spirit, give me insight and direction as I explore my past. What has energized me and what will guide me as I strive to fulfill my God-given calling and destiny?

Thank God for His GPS

In My Words

Have you ever been driving with a map you picked up at a gas station or map quest printout in hand, and found yourself lost when you made the wrong turn or reached an unexpected detour?

After you pulled over your vehicle, you started straightening out the map, walking your fingers over the map looking for an alternate route. Or you started reading the map quest printout to see what you missed, where you went wrong. If you used GPS or consulted Google Maps, you still would not have been 100% certain of reaching your destination.

Good thing we have God's GPS to help us in our Christian walk, God's Positioning System or God's Purposing System. Thank God for his GPS. It's 100% guaranteed. It tells us exactly where we are in our Christian walk as his sons and daughters, our position, and where we should be going, our purpose. He keeps us on the straight and narrow path if we follow the directions he gives us in his Word, through others, and in our prayer life.

God's GPS keeps us on the straight and narrow path.

Too bad Adam and Eve didn't have God's GPS and the ability to go before the Lord for directions. But didn't God give them directions? After all, they knew where they were and didn't have to go anywhere, did they? And God was very direct about what he expected of them.

In Genesis, we read about how God saw Adam needed a partner. He created Eve to meet that need. Adam and Eve were exactly where God wanted them to be and they knew their purpose. Then what does Adam do? Like a typical man

who never asks for directions, he listens to Eve instead of
listening to God. He disobeys God. The result? Adam and Eve
are lost, banished from the Garden because Adam made the
wrong decision. He made a wrong turn. He turned away from
God in disobedience when he bit into the apple from the Tree
of Knowledge.

We too make wrong decisions. We too take wrong turns.
We too disobey God. How do we keep on track in doing what
God wants us to do, in being the person God wants us to be?

Through his Word, through other people, and through the
work of the Holy Spirit, God helps us navigate our way
through life, overcoming obstacles, avoiding distractions,
making the right turns, making good decisions, and reversing
negative thinking. We have to tap into his GPS system. He
will not lead us astray.

I tell my life coaching clients that even though we explore
who they are and discover their God-given purpose during
our sessions, the exact path getting there and accomplishing
that purpose is subject to change and is in God's hands.

In God's Words

**Whether you turn to the right or to the left, your ears
will hear a voice behind you, saying, "This is the
way; walk in it."** (Isaiah 30:21)

**To shine on those living in darkness and in the
shadow of death to guide our feet into the path of
peace.** (Luke 1:79)

**If any of you lacks wisdom, you should ask God, who
gives generously to all without finding fault, and it
will be given to you.** (James 1:5)

Also read: Psalm 32:8, Psalm 37:23, Isaiah 48:17

In the Words of Others

"God's guidance is almost always step-by-step. He does not show us our life's plan all at once. Sometimes our anxiousness to know the will of God comes from a desire to peer over God's shoulder to see what His plan is. What we need to do is learn to trust Him to guide us." Jerry Bridges

"A God wise enough to create me and the world is wise enough to watch out for me." Philip Yancey

In Your Words

Have you ever felt lost, uncertain about where you were heading in life? If so, to whom did you turn for direction?

What do you do when making a major decision or you're facing challenges, unsure of where to turn? To whom or to what do you turn for direction?

Has prayer, God's Word, and time spent with him been part of your daily routine? Describe the difference it makes.

In Your Journal

Say It. Pray It. Share It.

Lord God, from the beginning of time you knew the path I would take in life. I pray that path will let me glorify you through service to others, and that I will trust in you.

God's Snow Plow Clears Your Way

In My Words

I woke up one morning to the sound of a snow plow clearing the road outside my house. "It's about time," I thought. We just experienced the first significant snow fall of the year.

A few minutes later, I settled in my favorite lounge chair to read a daily devotional from Sarah Young's book, *Jesus Calling*. The last sentence in the reading for that day read, "Hold My hand in deliberate dependence on Me, and I will smooth out the path before you."[6]

Coincidence?

I've not been very good over the years holding God's hand in deliberate dependence on him. Many times, it was more of a grasping for his hand when I really needed help, or I needed his intercession for someone else's problems. And I'm still a work in progress, reminding myself every day the Lord my God is ever present, ready to help.

The Lord drives a snow plow clearing a path for us.

Thinking back, I can recall instances when the road ahead of me looked pretty intimidating with personal and professional challenges. Metaphorically speaking, I was looking at a steep road ahead with seemingly insurmountably high snowdrifts. But somehow, I survived and even benefited in unexpected ways from those challenges as certain people entered my life at key times, as did fortuitous circumstances and events.

I can very easily picture how God, with his awesome power, steered a huge snow plow in front of me, smoothing out the path before me, and applying people, circumstances, and events to my challenges. After all, he guided the Israelites out of Egypt after 40 years of wandering, and led them across the Red Sea, after which they camped at Mount Sinai, where Moses received the Ten Commandments.

When you face challenges, it's important to remember how God goes before you. The Father already knows what you are facing and will face. He created you and knows every part of your being, past, present, and future. The Son, our Lord and Savior, walked this earth just like you and me. He was tempted like you and me. He understands what it is to be you and me. The Holy Spirit, the helper, was given to you and me as a direct link to Father. He intercedes for us and protects us, the Father's children.

As you wake up tomorrow, listen for the sound of the triune God smoothing out the path before you. You won't hear the sound of a snow plow scrapping a snow-covered road. But if you listen deep in your heart and soul, you'll hear the Lord saying, "I am in control." Embrace that sound of freedom throughout your day.

In God's Words

The name of the LORD is a fortified tower; the righteous run to it and are safe. (Proverbs 18:10)

The least of you will become a thousand, the smallest a mighty nation. I am the LORD; in its time I will do this swiftly. (Isaiah 60:22)

What, then, shall we say in response to these things? If God is for us, who can be against us? (Romans 8:31)

Also read: Psalm 27:1, Isaiah 54:17, 1 Corinthians 10:13

In the Words of Others

"Coincidence is God's way of remaining anonymous."
Albert Einstein

"Coincidences are spiritual puns." G.K. Chesterton

"Over every mountain there is a path, although it may not be seen from the valley." Theodore Roethke

"I did my best and God did the rest." Hattie McDaniel

In Your Words

Recall when you faced difficulties, and despite your worries, things turned out okay. What unexpected opportunities emerged, new doors opened, or dismissed opportunities reemerged?

What individuals had a positive influence on the situations? Why do you think they had a positive influence?

Do you recall praying about challenges you faced, asking the Lord for help? If yes, consider what role God may have played arranging people and events to influence the outcome.

In Your Journal

Say It. Pray It. Share It.

Lord Jesus, be with me at the start of each day and help me turn my day over to you, living confidently knowing you are in complete control.

How to Resurrect Dry Dream Bones

In My Words

I admit it. I was daydreaming during the church service on the Sunday a pastor preached a sermon on Ezekiel 37:1-4. I was thinking about dreams, the kind of dreams you and I have about what we want to accomplish in our personal and professional lives. I was thinking about unfulfilled dreams when he read the passage which vividly describes how the Lord led Ezekiel around a valley full of very dry bones and told him how to bring life to the bones.

Ezekiel writes, "Then he said to me, 'Prophesy over these bones, and say to them, O dry bones, hear the word of the Lord.'" I wondered how someone could prophesy over dead dreams to resurrect them. I considered how we could revisit dreams that were never fulfilled, and now lay forgotten and dead like dry bones in a deserted valley. How can you and I breathe new life into our dead dream bones and begin to flesh out the future?

Keep focused on actions to resurrect your dreams.

Our dreams die in stillbirth for the same reasons they are hard to resurrect once dead. Sometimes life gets in the way. Other times it's a negative cocktail of procrastination, anxiety and fear, wrong thinking and the wrong people, naysayers and critics, bad habits and poor planning.

Once you commit to resurrecting a dream, it's important not to procrastinate, but to keep focused on actions needed to realize your dream and not be sidetracked by accomplishing easier, more enjoyable tasks out of the lack of discipline, anxiety, or fear.

You'll also never find a shortage of those around you who will try to dampen your enthusiasm, criticize your plans, or steal your time and energy, asking you to get involved in their problems at the expense of accomplishing your priorities. It's important to be a good neighbor and fellow Christian. However, be wise in prayerfully setting limits.

Sometimes we can be our own worst enemy when we embark on fulfilling a dream. Wrong ideas and misconceptions about who we are and the way life works, birthed in our childhood and as we are socialized and experience the world, can negatively affect what we believe we can accomplish.

If bad habits and poor planning hampered your efforts to fulfill a dream, determine what habitual ways of thinking or acting were involved and avoid them. As you plan to avoid negative habits, set S.M.A.R.T. goals that are specific, measurable, attainable, relevant, and timely. Use positive affirmations to reignite the excitement of accomplishing your dream.

In the process of resurrecting a dream, ask the Holy Spirit for guidance and strength as you avoid influences that may have killed your dreams in the first place, and renew efforts to fulfill the dream. It could be it was the Lord's will that your dream was not to be. Ask the Holy Spirit to help you discern the Lord's will.

In God's Words

Then the LORD replied: "Write down the revelation and make it plain on tablets so that a herald may run with it. For the revelation awaits an appointed time; it speaks of the end and will not prove false. Though it lingers, wait for it; it will certainly come and will not delay." (Habakkuk 2:2-3)

He replied, "Because you have so little faith. Truly I tell you, if you have faith as small as a mustard seed, you can say to this mountain, 'Move from here to there,' and it will move. Nothing will be impossible for you." (Matthew 17:20)

Also read: Proverbs 3:5-6, Ezekiel 37:1-4, John 4:1

In the Words of others

"Not fulfilling your dreams will be a loss to the world, because the world needs everyone's gift---yours and mine." Barbara Sher

"Never give up on a dream just because of the time it will take to accomplish it. The time will pass anyway." Earl Nightingale

"Hold fast to dreams, for if dreams die, life is a broken-winged bird that cannot fly." Langston Hughes

In Your Words

Dig up an unfulfilled dream and think about it for a few quiet moments. Recall and relive the excitement and enthusiasm you once had thinking about fulfilling the dream.

As you listen to your lost dream story, recall reasons why you never fulfilled the dream. Imagine what could have happened had you fulfilled the dream.

Describe how to put flesh back on the dream with realistic S.M.A.R.T. goal setting and effective action, and with the help of the Holy Spirit.

Write three positive affirmations for the dream, breathing life into it as Ezekiel did, "prophesying" over the dry dream bones.

In Your Journal

Say It. Pray It. Share It.

Holy Spirit, I come before you holding dead dreams I would like to revive. I ask you to give me the wisdom, strength, and courage to bring them back to life.

Sea Glass Chronicles: Picking Up the Broken

In My Words

One of the activities I've become accustomed to when visiting a cottage on Lake Erie, is walking along the shore with my head down looking for sea glass, otherwise known as beach glass or drift glass. I find it fascinating so many people spend hours meandering along a beach at a snail's pace looking for colored pieces of glass washed up on shore.

Initially, I thought the glass pieces were remnants of bottles and glassware broken by visitors and tossed into the waters. But after researching on line, I discovered the pieces I collected could have been afloat for 30 to 40 years, maybe even 100 years.

As I fingered each piece of colored glass on a recent stay, I recalled how I also learned the pieces are given polished edges by the currents, and a frosted color by the presence of salt in the water. Whatever their original story might have been, part of clear glassware, an amber beer bottle, a blue liniment jar, or a black whisky jug from a 18th century sailing ship, each piece was destined to become part of new story thanks to me and others combing the beaches.

They were buffeted and broken by life's turbulence.

Early one morning, I scanned the horizon of the lake as I recalled meeting people over the years who had been buffeted, broken, and discolored by the turbulent waters of life. The loss of loved ones, job loss, debilitating sickness, extreme poverty, challenging addictions, and the effects of aging take their toll.

I also thought about how sea glass collectors and amateurs create new stories for the broken pieces of sea glass, using them to create chandeliers, mirrors, pictures and frames, sculptures, and even greeting cards. All the new creations made from broken bottles, jars, and glassware were made possible because people took the time to stop, sift through the sand, and pick up the glass.

It's easy and understandable to be so wrapped up in our own worlds, rushing here and there, attending to our own problems, that we pass over the broken pieces of humanity that surround us like broken pieces of sea glass on a beach.

It would have been perfectly understandable if the traveler we call the Good Samaritan had breezed on by the injured man alongside the road. He had places to go and things to do. But he stopped, had compassion on the man, bound his wounds, administered oil and wine, and took him to an inn. He even provided for the innkeeper's care of the man when he left.

The Samaritan stopped and picked up a broken piece of humanity passed over by others, and helped create a new story for a broken soul. He probably would have been a great sea glass collector. How about you?

In God's Words

There will always be poor people in the land. Therefore, I command you to be openhanded toward your fellow Israelites who are poor and needy in your land. (Deuteronomy 15:11)

"What should we do then?" the crowd asked. John answered, "Anyone who has two shirts should share with the one who has none, and anyone who has food should do the same." (Luke 3:10-11)

Also read: Proverbs 21:13, Luke 10:25-29, Philippians 2:4

In the Words of Others

"You have not lived today until you have done something for someone who can never repay you." John Bunyan

"I don't want to live in the kind of world where we don't look out for each other. Not just the people that are close to us, but anybody who needs a helping hand. I can't change the way anybody else thinks, or what they choose to do, but I can do my bit." Charles de Lint

"Love is not patronizing and charity isn't about pity, it is about love. Charity and love are the same -- with charity you give love, so don't just give money but reach out your hand instead." Mother Teresa

"No one is useless in this world who lightens the burdens of another." Charles Dickens

In Your Words

Describe a time when you had an opportunity to help someone who suffered a loss, was very sick, or fighting an addiction. What did you do?

Are you aware of a person who was buffeted, broken and discolored by life, and who survived and flourished with the help of others? If so, reflect on the story.

Search the scriptures for another example of a man or a woman who unexpectedly took the time and made the effort to help someone in distress.

In Your Journal

Say It. Pray It. Share It.

Lord Jesus, help me be the person who takes the time and makes the effort to stop and care for someone who needs help after being buffeted and broken by the challenges of life.

Priceless: The Price of Presence

In My Words

Have you ever visited a friend who was suffering the loss of a loved one, who just learned about a life-threatening illness, who was involved in a traumatic event, or who was experiencing trauma in their personal life? Were you speechless because you didn't know what to say or do?

Our natural reaction in situations like these is to try to do something for the person or tell them something, even give them advice. We prepare ourselves before visiting by planning what we will say, how we will act, what we will do. And there is nothing inherently wrong with this as it reflects our compassion and willingness to make ourselves vulnerable.

There are times when we have to be willing to just be present, really present in the moment, in a physical, emotional, and spiritual way. There are times when silence is golden, a simple hug comforting, spending time invaluable. The cost--priceless.

It's difficult to BE with someone who is hurting.

In pastoral care, we have a term for this willingness to simply be present alongside someone who is hurting. We refer to this as a ministry of presence. This ministry is by no means the exclusive domain of ministers, caregivers, and professionals. When a person visits someone who is hurting to offer comfort and support, and remains present without having to do or say something, they are performing a ministry of presence.

This type of ministry can be challenging. It seems contrary to our understandable desire to actively help, to do something to make things better, to say something appropriate that will make a difference. Just as it is hard to totally trust in God and not rely totally on our inadequate human efforts, it is difficult to simply BE present with someone who is hurting.

A good way to prepare before providing a ministry of presence is to focus more on the heart than the head. Your head tells you to intervene in some way, to say the right thing or even fix the situation. Your heart tells you that you simply need to be there, emotionally and lovingly, and not somewhere else. Most importantly, because of your natural tendency to intervene in some way, it's time to turn to God and trust his guidance.

Before I enter a room to visit a patient who is suffering and having spiritual distress, or sitting down with family members who are watching their loved one suffer or deal with their death, I ask the Holy Spirit to be present and give me guidance, not of the mind, but of the heart and soul. I prepare mentally, but in my heart and soul I turn my visit over to the Lord.

Remember, God gave us the ultimate example of being a ministry of presence when he chose to become human so we could say, "God is with us." Give what you can, even if it's only yourself in silence.

In God's Words

Carry each other's burdens, and in this way, you will fulfill the law of Christ. (Galatians 6:2)

Each of you must bring a gift in proportion to the way the LORD your God has blessed you. (Deuteronomy 16:17)

I needed clothes and you clothed me, I was sick and you looked after me, I was in prison and you came to visit me. (Matthew 25:36)

Also read: Proverbs 3:27, Colossians 3:12, Romans 12:15

In the Words of Others

"The friend who can be silent with us in a moment of despair or confusion, who can stay with us in an hour of grief and bereavement, who can tolerate not knowing...not healing, not curing...that is a friend who cares." Henri Nouwen

"Walking with a friend in the dark is better than walking alone in the light." Helen Keller

"Let every man abide in the calling wherein he is called and his work will be as sacred as the work of the ministry. It is not what a man does that determines whether his work is sacred or secular, it is why he does it." A.W. Tozer

In Your Words

Recall a time when you visited someone suffering or grieving and you didn't know what to say or how to act? What were your thoughts and emotions before the visit?

If you experienced a ministry of presence as described earlier, what were your thoughts during and after your visit?

What role do you see the Lord playing in visits that may require you to BE present with someone in silence and love?

In Your Journal

Say It. Pray It. Share It.

Holy Spirit, give me the wisdom to know what to do if I am called to perform a ministry of presence. Lord Jesus, give me the patience to simply BE your instrument of comfort and peace.

Tears of Sorrow, Tears of Joy

In My Words

In my years of visiting hospice patients and their families as a spiritual care coordinator for a senior health care system, I've had the privilege of being with family members at their loved one's bedside, visiting with them at funeral homes, conducting memorial and funeral services, and following up with them to address their bereavement concerns.

Due to the demographic of the patients I visit, I usually enter this sacred time and space of people who have walked this earth for 70 years or more, sometimes over 100 years. And due to the nature of the health system, founded by a religious order, the patients and their families usually have a deep faith.

The comment I often hear made by the grieving family members is that the passing of their loved one is a "mixed blessing," especially after months or years of suffering. I usually respond, "It's a time for tears of sorrow and tears of joy." Without exception, they agree.

Losing a loved one is undoubtedly a time to shed tears of sorrow. But why a time for tears of joy?

Can losing a loved one be a time for sorrow and joy?

When a younger person or someone in their prime dies, when death thrusts itself unexpectedly onto a family, or when violence takes a loved one, tears of joy, while still possible at some point depending on the depth of a family's faith, are far and few in between.

When an aged senior is living the last months, weeks, or days of his or her life, they have often lived a full life punctuated by frequent hospitalizations, physical and mental decline, and painful suffering. Family and friends are understandably torn between praying for recovery and praying for the Lord to take their loved one and friend home. In these instances, tears of joy more readily mix with those of sorrow.

Paraphrasing comments I've heard from family members over the years, they would say: "We will miss her, but she lived a long life. We are happy she is no longer suffering, and we know she is with the Lord. She is finally at peace." They often add their loved one will see family members and friends who have gone before them when they go to heaven. For these families, tears of sorrow were mixed with tears of joy.

In God's Words

The LORD is close to the brokenhearted and saves those who are crushed in spirit. (Psalm 34:18)

Praise be to the God and Father of our Lord Jesus Christ, the Father of compassion and the God of all comfort, who comforts us in all our troubles, so that we can comfort those in any trouble with the comfort we ourselves receive from God. (2 Corinthians 1:3-4)

He will wipe every tear from their eyes. There will be no more death or mourning or crying or pain, for the old order of things has passed away. (Revelation 21:4)

Also read: Ecclesiastes 3:1-14, John 3:16, Matthew 5:4

In the Words of Others

"Death is for many of us the gate of Hell; but we are inside on the way out, not outside on the way in."
George Bernard Shaw

"I look at life as a gift of God. Now that He wants it back I have no right to complain." Joyce Carey

"Do not seek death. Death will find you. But seek the road which makes death a fulfillment." Dag Hammarskjold

In Your Words

If you lost loved ones who were aged, seriously ill, and suffering, describe your feelings during their final days. Did you shed tears of sorrow and tears of joy?

How did your faith or lack of faith influence any of these experiences?

Read Psalm 23 and reflect on how it applied to your situation. Consider how it applies to your Christian walk.

In Your Journal

Say It. Pray It. Share It.

Lord Jesus, I thank you for the comfort and peace you give those who lose loved ones, assuring them their loved ones who left this world as your children, will be with you.

Notes

1. *Baltimore Catechism*, Lesson 1, Question 6. (1891)
2. Ibid., Lesson 1, Question 9.
3. Daniel Goldman, *Emotional Intelligence: Why It Can Matter More Than IQ* (New York: Bantam Books 1995).
4. Rick Warren, *The Purpose Driven Life: What on Earth Am I Here for?* (Michigan:Zondervan 2001), 276.
5. Daniel G. Amen M.D. *Change Your Brain Change Your Life: The Breakthrough Program for Conquering Anxiety, Depression, Obsessiveness, Anger and Impulsiveness* (Three Rivers Press: New York 1998)
6. Sarah Young, *Jesus Calling: Enjoying Peace in His Presence* (Thomas Nelson; Special and Rev edition: October 10, 2004)